D0835834

An Illustrated

Anthology of

War

Poems

Publisher and Creative Director: Nick Wells
Project Editor and Selection: Sara Robson
Designer: Nik Keevil

STAR FIRE BOOKS
Crabtree Hall, Crabtree Lane
Fulham, London SW6 6TY
United Kingdom

www.star-fire.co.uk

First published in 2006

06 08 10 09 07

1 3 5 7 9 10 8 6 4 2

Star Fire is part of The Foundry Creative Media Company Limited

© The Foundry 2006

A CIP record for this book is available from the British Library.

ISBN 1–84451–447–1

Every effort has been made to contact copyright holders. We apologize
in advance for any omissions and would be pleased to insert the
appropriate acknowledgement in subsequent editions of this publication.

While every endeavour has been made to ensure the accuracy of the
reproduction of the images in this book, we would be grateful to receive
any comments or suggestions for inclusion in future reprints.

Printed in China

Thanks to: Chris Herbert, Melinda Révész,
Rosanna Singler and Claire Walker

An Illustrated

Anthology of

War

Poems

STAR FIRE BOOKS

Contents

Introduction

War arouses a vast range of human emotions, from love of one's country and pride, to hatred and intense sorrow. It is no surprise, then, that it has been the subject for such an abundance of thoughtful and reflective poetry. The sheer number of ways in which it has been explored is no less impressive, from the intense and emotionally harrowing experiences of the individual soldier to the poems narrating battles in their entirety.

War poetry is no modern phenomenon – almost as old as war itself, it has been written about for centuries. Looking at this poetry through the ages, from poems about Viking battles in the eleventh century through to the First World War, this anthology allows the reader to see the shifts in the way that

war was understood and thought about. Poetry written before the First World War shows a more stoical attitude to war. The poets from these eras illustrate how society understood death and pain in war to be a necessary part of being human. Many believed that the point of war was to display courage and bravery in the face of adversity or impending death, in order to protect their country and the values that it stood for.

Several of the world's best-known and most well respected poets have dedicated themselves to the complex topic of war, including William Shakespeare (1564–1616), Geoffrey Chaucer (1343–1400), Lord Byron (1788–1824) and Wilfred Owen (1893–1918). Shakespeare displayed a more tolerant attitude to war. The great playwright made war a theme of many of his plays, using it to examine how his characters responded, seen best with King Henry in *Henry V*, and going on to examine how war affected society as a whole.

In contrast, poetry written around the First World War displays an attitude that has drastically shifted from this unquestioning acceptance of the cost of combat. The poetry focuses on the human toll of war, and how it affects the lives of the soldiers and their families left behind. This is not to say that poets are merely there to give opinions about the merits of war, positive or otherwise; rather the purpose of their poetry is to create a deeper understanding of the effects of war on those who partake in it. Furthermore, its purpose has become to add to mankind's understanding of human nature, exploring the misery and pain that humans are capable of inflicting on each other.

Wilfred Owen's poetry exemplifies this new emotional and subjective treatment. Like many of the poets of this period, Owen experienced war first-hand and reported on what he experienced rather than standing back and commenting from a distance, like many of the poets before him. This goes some way towards explaining the new personal style of poetry.

Organised by theme, this poetry anthology is divided into five sections that try to capture the many ways in which poets have portrayed this intriguing subject. From the outbreak of war through to peace and the aftermath of war, the verses included capture the essence of conflict through the thoughts of those influenced by or subject to it.

THE OUTBREAK OF WAR

The Battle of Maldon

…it was shatterd.
Then Brhytnoth ordered every warrior to dismount,
Let loose his horse and go forward into battle
With faith in his own skills and bravery.
Thus Offa's young son could not see for himself
That the earl was no man to suffer slackness.
He sent his best falcon flying from his wrist
To the safety of the forest and strode into the fight;
The boy's behaviour was a testament
That he would not be weak in the turmoil of battle.
Eadric too was firmly resolved to follow his leader
Into the fight. At once he hurried forward
With his spear. He feared no foe
For as long as he could lift his shield
And weild a sword: he kept his word
That he would pierce and parry before his prince.
Then Byrhtnoth began to martial his men.
He rode about, issuing instructions
As to how they should tightly grip their shields
Forgetting their qualms and pangs of fear.
And when he had arrayed the warriors' ranks
He dismounted with his escort at a carefully chosen place
Where his finest troops stood prepared to fight.

Anonymous (11th Century)

Extract from Henry V Act 3 Scene III

The gates of mercy shall be all shut up,
And the flesh'd soldier, rough and hard of heart,
In liberty of bloody hand shall range
With conscience wide as hell, mowing like grass
Your fresh-fair virgins and your flowering infants.
What is it then to me, if impious war,
Array'd in flames like to the prince of fiends,
Do, with his smirch'd complexion, all fell feats
Enlink'd to waste and desolation?
What is't to me, when you yourselves are cause,
If your pure maidens fall into the hand
Of hot and forcing violation?
What rein can hold licentious wickedness
When down the hill he holds his fierce career?
We may as bootless spend our vain command
Upon the enraged soldiers in their spoil
As send precepts to the leviathan
To come ashore. Therefore, you men of Harfleur,
Take pity of your town and of your people,
Whiles yet my soldiers are in my command;
Whiles yet the cool and temperate wind of grace
O'erblows the filthy and contagious clouds
Of heady murder, spoil and villany.
If not, why, in a moment look to see
The blind and bloody soldier with foul hand

Defile the locks of your shrill-shrieking daughters;
Your fathers taken by the silver beards,
And their most reverend heads dash'd to the walls,
Your naked infants spitted upon pikes,
Whiles the mad mothers with their howls confused
Do break the clouds, as did the wives of Jewry
At Herod's bloody-hunting slaughtermen.
What say you? will you yield, and this avoid,
Or, guilty in defence, be thus destroy'd?

William Shakespeare (1564–1616)

"YOUR COUNTRY NEEDS YOU"

St. Crispin's Day Speech from Henry V

WESTMORELAND. O that we now had here
But one ten thousand of those men in England
That do no work to-day!

KING. What's he that wishes so?
My cousin Westmoreland? No, my fair cousin;
If we are mark'd to die, we are enow
To do our country loss; and if to live,
The fewer men, the greater share of honour.
God's will! I pray thee, wish not one man more.
By Jove, I am not covetous for gold,
Nor care I who doth feed upon my cost;
It yearns me not if men my garments wear;
Such outward things dwell not in my desires.
But if it be a sin to covet honour,
I am the most offending soul alive.
No, faith, my coz, wish not a man from England.
God's peace! I would not lose so great an honour
As one man more methinks would share from me
For the best hope I have. O, do not wish one more!
Rather proclaim it, Westmoreland, through my host,
That he which hath no stomach to this fight,
Let him depart; his passport shall be made,
And crowns for convoy put into his purse;
We would not die in that man's company
That fears his fellowship to die with us.
This day is call'd the feast of Crispian.
He that outlives this day, and comes safe home,
Will stand a tip-toe when this day is nam'd,

And rouse him at the name of Crispian.
He that shall live this day, and see old age,
Will yearly on the vigil feast his neighbours,
And say "To-morrow is Saint Crispian."
Then will he strip his sleeve and show his scars,
And say "These wounds I had on Crispian's day."
Old men forget; yet all shall be forgot,
But he'll remember, with advantages,
What feats he did that day. Then shall our names,
Familiar in his mouth as household words-
Harry the King, Bedford and Exeter,
Warwick and Talbot, Salisbury and Gloucester-
Be in their flowing cups freshly rememb'red.
This story shall the good man teach his son;
And Crispin Crispian shall ne'er go by,
From this day to the ending of the world,
But we in it shall be remembered-
We few, we happy few, we band of brothers;
For he to-day that sheds his blood with me
Shall be my brother; be he ne'er so vile,
This day shall gentle his condition;
And gentlemen in England now-a-bed
Shall think themselves accurs'd they were not here,
And hold their manhoods cheap whiles any speaks
That fought with us upon Saint Crispin's day.

William Shakespeare (1564–1616)

21

The Drum

I hate that drum's discordant sound,
Parading round, and round, and round:
To thoughtless youth it pleasure yields,
And lures from cities and from fields,
To sell their liberty for charms
Of tawdry lace, and glittering arms;
And when Ambition's voice commands,
To march, and fight, and fall, in foreign lands.

I hate that drum's discordant sound,
Parading round, and round, and round:
To me it talks of ravaged plains,
And burning towns, and ruined swains,
And mangled limbs, and dying groans,
And widow's tears, and orphan's moans;
And all that Misery's hand bestows,
To fill the catalogue of human woes.

John Scott of Amwell (1730–83)

A War Song to Englishmen

Prepare, prepare the iron helm of war,
Bring forth the lots, cast in the spacious orb;
Th' Angel of Fate turns them with mighty hands,
And casts them out upon the darken'd earth!
Prepare, prepare!
Prepare your hearts for Death's cold hand! prepare
Your souls for flight, your bodies for the earth;
Prepare your arms for glorious victory;
Prepare your eyes to meet a holy God!
Prepare, prepare!
Whose fatal scroll is that? Methinks 'tis mine!
Why sinks my heart, why faltereth my tongue?
Had I three lives, I'd die in such a cause,
And rise, with ghosts, over the well-fought field.
Prepare, prepare!
The arrows of Almighty God are drawn!
Angels of Death stand in the louring heavens!
Thousands of souls must seek the realms of light,
And walk together on the clouds of heaven!
Prepare, prepare!
Soldiers, prepare! Our cause is Heaven's cause;
Soldiers, prepare! Be worthy of our cause:
Prepare to meet our fathers in the sky:
Prepare, O troops, that are to fall to-day!
Prepare, prepare!

Alfred shall smile, and make his harp rejoice;
The Norman William, and the learnèd Clerk,
And Lion Heart, and black-brow'd Edward, with
His loyal queen, shall rise, and welcome us!
Prepare, prepare!

William Blake (1757–1827)

Alteration of the Old Ballad "Amator Patriae"
("Ye Gentlemen of England.")

Composed on the Prospect of a Russian War.

Ye Mariners of England
That guard our native Seas,
Whose Flag has brav'd a thousand years,
The Battle and the Breeze,
Your glorious Standard launch again,
To match another Foe,
And sweep thro' the Deep
While the Stormy Tempests blow—.
While the Battle rages loud and long
And the Stormy Tempests blow!
The Spirits of your Fathers
Shall start from ev'ry wave;
For the Deck it was their Field of Fame
And Ocean was their Grave!
Where BLAKE (the Boast of Freedom) fell
Your manly hearts shall glow,
As ye sweep thro' the Deep
When the stormy Tempests blow—
When the Battle rages loud and long—
And the stormy tempests blow!

BRITANNIA needs no Bulwark,
No Tow'rs along the Steep;
Her march is o'er the mountain-waves,
Her home is on the Deep:—
With thunders from her native Oak

She quells the floods below,
As they roar on the shore
When the stormy Tempests blow—
When the Battle rages loud and long
And the stormy Tempests blow!

The Meteor Flag of England
Must yet terrific burn,
Till Danger's troubled Night depart
And the Star of Peace return!
Then, then, ye Ocean Warriors,
Our Song and Feast shall flow
To the fame of your name,
When the Tempests cease to blow—
When the fiery fight is heard no more
And the Tempests cease to blow!

Thomas Campbell (1777–1844)

Extract from Childe Harold's Pilgrimage

There was a sound of revelry by night,
And Belgium's Capital had gathered then
Her beauty and her Chivalry, and bright
The lamps shone o'er fair women and brave men;
A thousand hearts beat happily; and when
Music arose with its voluptuous swell,
Soft eyes looked love to eyes which spake again,
And all went merry as a marriage bell;
But hush! a deep sound strikes like a rising knell!

Did ye not hear it?—No; 'twas but the wind,
Or the car rattling o'er the stony street;
On with the dance! let joy be unconfined;
No sleep till morn, when Youth and Pleasure meet
To chase the glowing Hours with flying feet—
But hark!—that heavy sound breaks in once more,
As if the clouds its echo would repeat;
And nearer, clearer, deadlier than before!
Arm! Arm! it is—it is—the cannon's opening roar!

Within a windowed niche of that high hall
Sate Brunswick's fate chieftain; he did hear
That sound the first amidst the festival,
And caught its tone with Death's prophetic ear;
And when they smiled because he deemed it near,
His heart more truly knew that peal too well
Which stretched his father on a bloody bier,
And roused the vengeance blood alone could quell;
He rushed into the field, and, foremost fighting, fell.

Ah! then and there was hurrying to and fro,
And gathering tears, and tremblings of distress,
And cheeks all pale, which but an hour ago
Blushed at the praise of their own loveliness;
And there were sudden partings, such as press
The life from out young hearts, and choking sighs
Which ne'er might be repeated; who could guess
If ever more should meet those mutual eyes,
Since upon night so sweet such awful morn could rise!

And there was mounting in hot haste: the steed,
The mustering squadron, and the clattering car,
Went pouring forward with impetuous speed,
And swiftly forming the ranks of war;
And deep thunder peal on pear afar;
And near, the beat of the alarming drum
Roused up the soldier ere the morning star;
While thronged the citizens with terror dumb,
Or whispering, with white lips–'The foe! They come! they come!

And wild and high the 'Cameron's Gathering' rose!
The war-note of Lochiel, which Albyn's hills
Have heard, and heard, too, have her Saxon foes:–
How in the noon ofnight that pibroch thrills,
Savage and shrill! But with the breath which fills
Their mountain-pipe, so fill the mountaineers
With the fierce native daring which instills
The stirring memory of a thousand years,
And Evan's, Donald's fame rings in each clansman's ears!

And Ardennes waves above them her green leaves,
Dewy with nature's tear drops, as they pass,
Grieving, if aught inanimate e'er grieves,
Over the unreturning brave,–alas!
Ere evening to be trodden like the grass
Which now beneath them, but above shall grow
In its next verdure, when this fiery mass
Of living valour, rolling on the foe
And burning with high hope, shall moulder cold and low.

Last noon beheld them full of lusty life,
Last eve in Beauty's circle proudly gay,
The midnight brought the signal-sound of strife,
The morn the marshalling in arms,–the day
Battle's magnificently-stern array!
The thunder-clouds close o'er it, which when rent
The earth is covered thick with other clay
Which her own clay shall cover, heaped and pent,
Rider and horse, –friend, foe, –in one red burial blent!

George Gordon, Lord Byron (1788–1824)

Extract from Don Juan

I WANT a hero: an uncommon want,
When every year and month sends forth a new one,
Till, after cloying the gazettes with cant,
The age discovers he is not the true one;
Of such as these I should not care to vaunt,
I'll therefore take our ancient friend Don Juan-
We all have seen him, in the pantomime,
Sent to the devil somewhat ere his time.

Vernon, the butcher Cumberland, Wolfe, Hawke,
Prince Ferdinand, Granby, Burgoyne, Keppel, Howe,
Evil and good, have had their tithe of talk,
And fill'd their sign posts then, like Wellesley now;
Each in their turn like Banquo's monarchs stalk,
Followers of fame, 'nine farrow' of that sow:
France, too, had Buonaparte and Dumourier
Recorded in the Moniteur and Courier.

Barnave, Brissot, Condorcet, Mirabeau,
Petion, Clootz, Danton, Marat, La Fayette,
Were French, and famous people, as we know:
And there were others, scarce forgotten yet,
Joubert, Hoche, Marceau, Lannes, Desaix, Moreau,
With many of the military set,
Exceedingly remarkable at times,
But not at all adapted to my rhymes.

Nelson was once Britannia's god of war,
And still should be so, but the tide is turn'd;
There's no more to be said of Trafalgar,
'T is with our hero quietly inurn'd;
Because the army's grown more popular,
At which the naval people are concern'd;
Besides, the prince is all for the land-service,
Forgetting Duncan, Nelson, Howe, and Jervis.

Brave men were living before Agamemnon
And since, exceeding valorous and sage,
A good deal like him too, though quite the same none;
But then they shone not on the poet's page,
And so have been forgotten:- I condemn none,
But can't find any in the present age
Fit for my poem (that is, for my new one);
So, as I said, I'll take my friend Don Juan.

George Gordon, Lord Byron (1788–1824)

Channel Firing

That night your great guns, unawares,
Shook all our coffins as we lay,
And broke the chancel window-squares,
We thought it was the Judgment-day
And sat upright. While drearisome
Arose the howl of wakened hounds:
The mouse let fall the altar-crumb,
The worms drew back into the mounds,
The glebe cow drooled. Till God called, "No;
It's gunnery practice out at sea
Just as before you went below;
The world is as it used to be:

"All nations striving strong to make
Red war yet redder. Mad as hatters
They do no more for Christés sake
Than you who are helpless in such matters.

"That this is not the judgment-hour
For some of them's a blessed thing,
For if it were they'd have to scour
Hell's floor for so much threatening ....

"Ha, ha. It will be warmer when
I blow the trumpet (if indeed
I ever do; for you are men,
And rest eternal sorely need)."

So down we lay again. "I wonder,
Will the world ever saner be,"
Said one, "than when He sent us under
In our indifferent century!"

And many a skeleton shook his head.
"Instead of preaching forty year,"
   My neighbour Parson Thirdly said,
"I wish I had stuck to pipes and beer."
   Again the guns disturbed the hour,
Roaring their readiness to avenge,
As far inland as Stourton Tower,
And Camelot, and starlit Stonehenge.

Thomas Hardy (1840–1928)

"Men who March Away"

Song of the Soldiers

WHAT of the faith and fire within us
Men who march away
Ere the barn-cocks say
Night is growing gray,
To hazards whence no tears can win us;
What of the faith and fire within us
Men who march away!

Is it a purblind prank, O think you,
Friend with the musing eye
Who watch us stepping by,
With doubt and dolorous sigh?
Can much pondering so hoodwink you?
Is it a purblind prank, O think you,
Friend with the musing eye?

Nay. We see well what we are doing,
Though some may not see —
Dalliers as they be —
England's need are we;
Her distress would leave us rueing:
Nay. We well see what we are doing,
Though some may not see!

In our heart of hearts believing
Victory crowns the just,
And that braggarts must

Surely bite the dust,
Press we to the field ungrieving,
In our heart of hearts believing
Victory crowns the just.

Hence the faith and fire within us
Men who march away
Ere the barn-cocks say
Night is growing gray,
To hazards whence no tears can win us;
Hence the faith and fire within us
Men who march away.

Thomas Hardy (1840–1928)

The Departure

Here, where Vespasian's legions struck the sands,
And Cedric with his Saxons entered in,
And Henry's army leapt afloat to win
Convincing triumphs over neighbour lands,
Vaster battalions press for further strands,
To argue in the selfsame bloody mode
Which this late age of thought, and pact, and code,
Still fails to mend. – Now deckward tramp the bands,
Yellow as autumn leaves, alive as spring;
And as each host draws out upon the sea
Beyond which lies the tragical To-be,
None dubious of the cause, none murmuring,
Wives, sisters, parents, wave white hands and smile,
As if they knew not that they weep the while.

Thomas Hardy (1840–1928)

The Call

Hark! 'tis the rush of the horses,
The crash of the galloping gun!
The stars are out of their courses;
The hour of Doom has begun.
Leap from thy scabbard, O sword!
Leap! 'Tis the Day of the Lord!
Prate not of peace any longer,
Laughter and idlesse and ease!
Up, every man that is stronger!
Leave but the priest on his knees!
Quick, every hand to the hilt!
Who striketh not—his the guilt!
Call not each man on his brother!
Cry not to Heaven to save!
Thou art the man—not another—
Thou, to off glove and out glaive!
Fight, ye who ne'er fought before!
Fight, ye old fighting-men more!

Francis William Bourdillon (1852–1921)

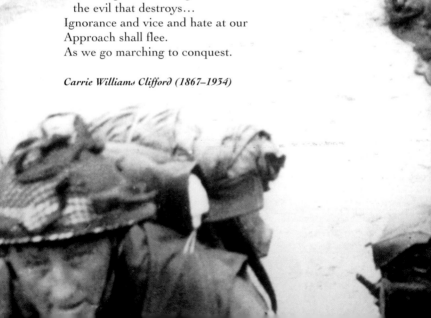

Marching to Conquest

We are battling for the right with
    purpose strong and true,
Tis a mighty struggle, but we've
    pledged to dare and do;
Pledged to conquer evil, and we'll see
    the conflict thro',
Marching and marching to conquest.
All the noble things of life we'll teach
    our girls and boys,
Warn them of its pitfalls, and reveal
    its purest joys;
Counsel, guide and keep them from
    the evil that destroys…
Ignorance and vice and hate at our
Approach shall flee.
As we go marching to conquest.

Carrie Williams Clifford (1867–1934)

Fall In

What will you lack sonny, what will you lack
When the girls line up on the street,
Shouting their love to the lads come back
From the foe they rushed to beat?
Will you send a strangled cheer to the sky
And grin till tour cheeks are red?
But what will you lack when your mate goes by
With a girl who cuts you dead?

Where will you look, sonny, where will you look
When your children yet to be
Clamour to learn of the part you took
In the War that kept men free?
Will you say it was naught to you if France
Stood up to her foe or bunked?
But where will you look when they give you the glance
That tells you they know you funked?

How will you fare, sonny, how will you fare
In the far-off winter night,
When you sit by the fire in an old man's chair
And your neighbours talk of the fight
Will you slink away, as it were from a blow,
Your old head shamed and bent?
Or, say – I was not with the first to go,
But I went, thank God, I went?

Why do they call, sonny, why do they call
For men, who are brave and strong?

It is naught to you if your country fall,
And Right is smashed by Wrong?
It is football still and the picture show,
The pub and the betting odds,
When your brothers stand to the tyrant's blow
And Britain's call is God's?

Harold Begbie (1871–1929)

The Last Evening

And night and distant rumbling; now the army's
carrier-train was moving out, to war.
He looked up from the harpsichord, and as
he went on playing, he looked across at her

almost as one might gaze into a mirror:
so deeply was her every feature filled
with his young features, which bore his pain and were
more beautiful and seductive with each sound.

Then, suddenly, the image broke apart.
She stood, as though distracted, near the window
and felt the violent drum-beats of her heart.

His playing stopped. From outside, a fresh wind blew.
And strangely alien on the mirror-table
stood the black shack with its ivory skull.

Rainer Maria Rilke (1875–1926)

This Is No Case of Petty Right or Wrong

This is no case of petty right or wrong
That politicians or philosophers
Can judge. I hate not Germans, nor grow hot
With love of Englishmen, to please newspapers.
Beside my hate for one fat patriot
My hatred of the Kaiser is love true:–
A kind of god he is, banging a gong.
But I have not to choose between the two,
Or between justice and injustice. Dinned
With war and argument I read no more
Than in the storm smoking along the wind
Athwart the wood. Two witches' cauldrons roar.
From one the weather shall rise clear and gay;
Out of the other an England beautiful
And like her mother that died yesterday.

Little I know or care if, being dull,
I shall miss something that historians
Can rake out of the ashes when perchance
The phoenix broods serene above their ken.
But with the best and meanest Englishmen
I am one in crying, God save England, lest
We lose what never slaves and cattle blessed.
The ages made her that made us from dust:
She is all we know and live by, and we trust
She is good and must endure, loving her so:
And as we love ourselves we hate our foe.

Edward Thomas (1878–1917)

The Trumpet

Rise up, rise up,
And, as the trumpet blowing
Chases the dreams of men,
As the dawn glowing
The stars that left unlit
The land and water,
Rise up and scatter
The dew that covers
The print of last night's lovers –
Scatter it, scatter it!

While you are listening
To the clear horn,
Forget, men, everything
On this earth newborn,
Except that it is lovelier
Than any mysteries.
Open your eyes to the air
That has washed the eyes of the stars
Through all the dewy night:
Up with the light,
To the old wars;
Arise, arise!

Edward Thomas (1878–1917)

Youth in Arms

HAPPY boy, happy boy,
David the immortal-willed,
Youth a thousand thousand times
Slain, but not once killed,
Swaggering again today
In the old contemptuous way;

Leaning backward from your thigh
Up against the tinselled bar—
Dust and ashes! is it you?
Laughing, boasting, there you are!
First we hardly recognized you
In your modern avatar.

Soldier, rifle, brown khaki—
Is your blood as happy so?
Where's your sling or painted shield,
Helmet, pike or bow?
Well, you're going to the wars –
That is all you need to know.

Graybeards plotted. They were sad.
Death was in their wrinkled eyes.
At their tables—with their maps,
Plans and calculations – wise
They all seemed; for well they knew
How ungrudgingly Youth dies.

At their green official baize
They debated all the night
Plans for your adventurous days
Which you followed with delight,
Youth in all your wanderings,
David of a thousand slings.

Harold Monro (1879–1932)

Youth in Arms II: Soldier

Are you going? To-night we must hear all your laughter;
We shall need to remember it in the quiet days after.
Lift your rough hands, grained like unpolished oak.
Drink, call, lean forward, tell us some happy joke.
Let us know every whim of your brain and innocent soul.
Your speech is let loose; your great loafing words roll
Like hill-waters. But every syllable said
Brings you nearer the time you'll be found lying dead
In a ditch, or rolled stiff on the stones of a plain.
(Thought! Thought go back into your kennel again:
Hound back!) Drink your glass, happy soldier, to-night.
Death is quick; you will laugh as you march to the fight.
We are wrong. Dreaming ever, we falter and pause:
You go forward unharmed without Why or Because.
Spring does not question. The war is like rain;
You will fall in the field like a flower without pain;
And who shall have noticed one sweet flower that dies?
The rain comes; the leaves open, and other flowers rise.

Harold Monro (1879–1932)

The Poets are Waiting

To what God
Shall we chant
Our songs of Battle?

The professional poets
Are measuring their thoughts
For felicitous sonnets;
They try them and fit them
Like honest tailors
Cutting materials
For fashion-plate suits.

The unprofessional
Little singers,
Most intellectual,
Merry with gossip,
Heavy with cunning,
Whose tedious brains are draped
In sultry palls of hair,
Reclining as usual
On armchairs and sofas,
Are grinning and gossiping,
Cake at their elbows –
They will not write us verses for the time;
Their storms are brewed in teacups and their wars
Are fought in sneers or little blots of ink.

To what God
Shall we chant
Our songs of Battle?

Hefty barbarians,
Roaring for war,
Are breaking upon us;
Clouds of their cavalry,
Waves of their infantry,
Mountains of guns.
Winged they are coming,
Plated and mailed,
Snorting their jargon.
Oh to whom shall a song of battle be chanted?

Not to our lord of the hosts on his ancient throne,
Drowsing the ages out in Heaven
The celestial choirs are mute, the angels have fled:
Word is gone forth abroad that our lord is dead.

To what God shall we chant
Our songs
Of battle?

Harold Monro (1879–1932)

Happy is England Now

There is not anything more wonderful
Than a great people moving towards the deep
Of an unguessed and unfeared future; nor
Is aught so dear of all held dear before
As the new passion stirring in their veins
When the destroying Dragon wakes from sleep.
Happy is England now, as never yet!
And though the sorrows of the slow days fret
Her faithfullest children, grief itself is proud.
Ev'n the warm beauty of this spring and summer
That turns to bitterness turns then to gladness
Since for this England the beloved ones died.
Happy is England in the brave that die
For wrongs not hers and wrongs so sternly hers;
Happy in those that give, give, and endure
The pain that never the new years may cure;
Happy in all her dark woods, green fields, towns,
Her hills and rivers and her chafing sea.
What'er was dear before is dearer now.
There's not a bird singing upon his bough
But sings the sweeter in our English ears:
There's not a nobleness of heart, hand, brain
But shines the purer; happiest is England now
In those that fight, and watch with pride and tears.

John Freeman (1880–1929)

Marching Men

Under the level winter sky
I saw a thousand Christs go by.
They sang an idle song and free
As they went up to calvary.
Careless of eye and coarse of lip,
They marched in holiest fellowship.
That heaven might heal the world, they gave
Their earth-born dreams to deck the grave.
With souls unpurged and steadfast breath
They supped the sacrament of death.
And for each one, far off, apart,
Seven swords have rent a woman's heart.

Marjorie Pickthall (1883–1922)

I Peace

Now, God be thanked Who has matched us with His hour,
And caught our youth, and wakened us from sleeping,
With hand made sure, clear eye, and sharpened power,
To turn, as swimmers into cleanness leaping,
Glad from a world grown old and cold and weary,
Leave the sick hearts that honour could not move,
And half-men, and their dirty songs and dreary,
And all the little emptiness of love!

Oh! we, who have known shame, we have found release there,
Where there's no ill, no grief, but sleep has mending,
Naught broken save this body, lost but breath;
Nothing to shake the laughing heart's long peace there
But only agony, and that has ending;
And the worst friend and enemy is but Death.

Rupert Brooke (1887–1915)

II Safety

Dear! of all happy in the hour, most blest
He who has found our hid security,
Assured in the dark tides of the world that rest,
And heard our word, 'Who is so safe as we?'
We have found safety with all things undying,
The winds, and morning, tears of men and mirth,
The deep night, and birds singing, and clouds flying,
And sleep, and freedom, and the autumnal earth.
We have built a house that is not for Time's throwing.
We have gained a peace unshaken by pain for ever.
War knows no power. Safe shall be my going,
Secretly armed against all death's endeavour;
Safe though all safety's lost; safe where men fall;
And if these poor limbs die, safest of all.

Rupert Brooke (1887–1915)

On Receiving the First News of the War

Snow is a strange white word.
No ice or frost
Has asked of bud or bird
For Winter's cost.

Yet ice and frost and snow
From earth to sky
This Summer land doth know.
No man knows why.

In all men's hearts it is.
Some spirit old
Hath turned with malign kiss
Our lives to mould.

Red fangs have torn His face.
God's blood is shed.
He mourns from His lone place
His children dead.

O! ancient crimson curse!
Corrode, consume.
Give back this universe
Its pristine bloom.

Isaac Rosenberg (1890–1918)

Soldier: Twentieth Century

I love you, great new Titan!
Am I not you?
Napoleon and Caesar
Out of you grew.

Out of unthinkable torture,
Eyes kissed by death,
Won back to the world again,
Lost and won in a breath,

Cruel men are made immortal,
Out of your pain born.
They have stolen the sun's power
With their feet on your shoulders worn.

Let them shrink from your girth,
That has outgrown the pallid days,
When you slept like Circe's swine,
Or a word in the brain's ways.

Isaac Rosenberg (1890–1918)

Recruiting

'Lads, you're wanted, go and help,'
On the railway carriage wall
Stuck the poster, and I thought
Of the hands that penned the call.

Fat civilians wishing they
'Could go out and fight the Hun.'
Can't you see them thanking God
That they're over forty-one?

Girls with feathers, vulgar songs –
Washy verse on England's need –
God – and don't we damned well know
How the message ought to read.

'Lads, you're wanted! over there,'
Shiver in the morning dew,
More poor devils like yourselves
Waiting to be killed by you.

Go and help to swell the names
In the casualty lists.
Help to make a column's stuff
For the blasted journalists.

Help to keep them nice and safe
From the wicked German foe.
Don't let him come over here!
'Lads, you're wanted – out you go.'

There's a better word than that,
Lads, and can't you hear it come
From a million men that call
You to share their martyrdom.

Leave the harlots still to sing
Comic songs about the Hun,
Leave the fat old men to say
Now *we've* go them on the run.

Better twenty honest years
Than their dull three score and ten.
Lads, you're wanted. Come and learn
To live and die with honest men.

You shall learn what men can do
If you will but pay the price,
Learn the gaiety and strength
In the gallant sacrifice.

Take your risk of life and death
Underneath the open sky.
Leave clean or go out quick –
Lads, you're wanted. Come and die.

E. A. Mackintosh (1893–1917)

Arms and the Boy

Let the boy try along this bayonet-blade
How cold steel is, and keen with hunger of blood;
Blue with all malice, like a madman's flash;
And thinly drawn with famishing for flesh.
Lend him to stroke these blind, blunt bullet-heads
Which long to muzzle in the hearts of lads.
Or give him cartridges of fine zinc teeth,
Sharp with the sharpness of grief and death.
For his teeth seem for laughing round an apple.
There lurk no claws behind his fingers supple;
And God will grow no talons at his heels,
Nor antlers through the thickness of his curls.

Wilfred Owen (1893–1918)

The Send-off

Down the close, darkening lanes they sang their way
To the siding-shed,
And lined the train with faces grimly gay.

Their breasts were stuck all white with wreath and spray
As men's are, dead.

Dull porters watched them, and a casual tramp
Stood staring hard,
Sorry to miss them from the upland camp.
Then, unmoved, signals nodded, and a lamp
Winked to the guard.

So secretly, like wrongs hushed-up, they went.
They were not ours:
We never heard to which front these were sent.

Nor there if they yet mock what women meant
Who gave them flowers.

Shall they return to beatings of great bells
In wild trainloads?
A few, a few, too few for drums and yells,
May creep back, silent, to still village wells
Up half-known roads.

Wilfred Owen (1893–1918)

To Germany

You are blind like us. Your hurt no man designed,
And no man claimed the conquest of your land.
But gropers both through fields of thought confined
We stumble and we do not understand.
You only saw your future bigly planned,
And we, the tapering paths of our own mind,
And in each other's dearest ways we stand,
And hiss and hate. And the blind fight the blind.
When it is peace, then we may view again
With new-won eyes each other's truer form
And wonder. Grown more loving-kind and warm
We'll grasp firm hands and laugh at the old pain,
When it is peace. But until peace, the storm
The darkness and the thunder and the rain.

Charles Hamilton Sorley (1895–1915)

"All the Hills and Vales Along"

ALL the hills and vales along
Earth is bursting into song,
And the singers are the chaps
Who are going to die perhaps.
O sing, marching men,
Till the valleys ring again.
Give your gladness to earth's keeping,
So be glad, when you are sleeping.

Cast away regret and rue,
Think what you are marching to
Little live, great pass.
Jesus Christ and Barabbas
Were found the same day.
This died, that went his way.
So sing with joyful breath.
For why, you are going to death.
Teeming earth will surely store
All the gladness that you pour.

Earth that never doubts nor fears,
Earth that knows of death, not tears,
Earth that bore with joyful ease
Hemlock for Socrates,
Earth that blossomed and was glad
'Neath the cross that Christ had,
Shall rejoice and blossom too
When the bullet reaches you.
Wherefore, men marching

On the road to death, sing!
Pour your gladness on earth's head,
So be merry, so be dead.

From the hills and valleys earth
Shouts back the sound of mirth,
Tramp of feet and lilt of song
Ringing all the road along.
All the music of their going,
Ringing, swinging, glad song-throwing,
Earth will echo still, when foot
Lies numb and voice mute.
On, marching men, on
To the gates of death with song.
Sow your gladness for earth's reaping,
So you may be glad, though sleeping.
Strew your gladness on earth's bed,
So be merry, so be dead.

Charles Hamilton Sorley (1895–1915)

Dauntless Dan

The cry went up for volunteers
To join the battle van
And then we gave three lusty cheers
And said here's Dauntless Dan!
For years upon the football field
He's been well to the fore
But to no living man he'll yield
In hatred of the Boer
They tried his ardour for to damp
By regulations stringent
But now he's in the Newtown Camp
Among the Fifth Contingent
They took him to the rifle butts
To try how he could aim
Although they said both eyes he shut
He got there all the same
He passed well through the riding test
Without a single spill
And now he ranks among the best
Does the Dauntless Dan McGill

Maurice McGill (fl. 1899–1902)

EVERYDAY LIFE IN WARTIME

Extract from The Knight's Tale

But in the dome of might Mars the red
With different figures all the sides wre spread;
This temple, less in form, with equal grace,
Ws imitative of the first in Thrace:
For that cold region was the loved abode
And sovereign mansion of the warrior god.
The landscape was a forest wide and bare,
Where neither beast nor humankind repair;
The fowl that scent afar the borders fly,
And shun the bitter blast, and wheel about the sky.
A cake of scurf lies baking on the groun,
And prickly stubs, instead of trees, are found;
Or woods with knots and knares deformed and old;
Headless the most, and hideous to behold:
A rattling tempest through he branches went,
That stripped 'em bare, and one sole way they bent.
Heaven froze above, severe; the clouds congeal,
And through the crystal vault appeared the standing hail.
Such was the face without:a mountain stood
Threatening from high, and overlooked the wood;
Beneath the lowering brow, and on a bent,
The temple stood of Mars armipotent:
The frame of burnished steel, that cast a glare
From far, and seemed to thaw the freezing air.
A strait, long entry to the temple led,
Blind with high walls, and horror overhead:
Thence issued such a blast and hollow roar,
As threatened from the hinge to heave the door.

Dsin que bon
nourables et
nobles auen
tures faittes

et Recorder hystoires z matiere
de grant science. Laquelle se
deuise en quatre parties
Mais ains que ie la comm

In through that door, a northern light there shone;
'Twas all it had, for windows there were none.
The gate was adamant; eternal frame!
Which, hewed by Mars himself, from Indian quarries came,
The labour of a god; and all along
Tough iron plates were clenched to make it strong.
A tun about was every pillar there;
A polished mirror shone not half so clear.
There saw I how the secret felon wrought,
And treason labouring in the traitor's thought,
And midwife Time the ripened plot to murder brought.
There red Anger dared the pallid Fear;
Next stood Hypocrisy, with holy leer;
Soft smiling, and demurely looking down,
But hid the dagger underneath the gown:
Th' assassinating wife, the household fiend;
And, far the blackest there, the traitor-friend.
On t'other side there stood Destruction bare;
Unpunished Rapine, and a waste of war;
Contest, with sharpened knives, in cloisters drawn,
And all with blood bespread the holy lawn.
Loud menaces were heard, and foul disgrace,
And bawling infamy, in language base;
Till sense was lost in sound, and silence fed the place.
The slayer of himself yet saw I there;
The gore congealed was clottered in his hair:
With eyes half closed and gaping mouth he lay,
And grim, as when he breathed his sullen soul away.
In midst of all the dome Misfortune sat,
And gloomy Discontent, and fell Debate,
And Madness laughing in his ireful mood,

And armed complaint on theft, and cries of blood.
There was the murdered corpse, in covert laid,
And violent death in thousand shapes displayed;
The city to the soldier's rage resigned;
Successless wars, and poverty behind;
Ships burnt in fight, or forced on rocky shores,
And the rash hunter strangled by the boars;
The newborn baby by nurses overlaid;
And the cook caught within the raging fire he made.
All ills of Mars his nature, flame, and steel;
The grasping charioteer, beneath the wheel
Of his own car, the ruined house that falls
And intercepts her lord betwixt the walls;
The whole division that to Mars pertains,
All trades of death that deal in steel for gains,
Were there:t he butcher, armourer, and smith,
Who forges sharpened fauchions, or the scythe.
The scarlet conquest on a tower was placed,
With shouts and soldier's acclamations graced;
A pointed sword hung threatening o'er his ead,
Sustained but by a slender wine of thread.
There saw I Mars his ides, the Capitol,
The seer in vain foretelling Caesar's fall;
The last triumvirs, and the wars they move,
And Antony, who lost the world for love.
These, and a thousand more, the fane adorn;
Their fates were painted ere the men were born,
All copied from the heavens, and ruling force
Of the red star, in his revolving course.

Geoffrey Chaucer (1343–1400)

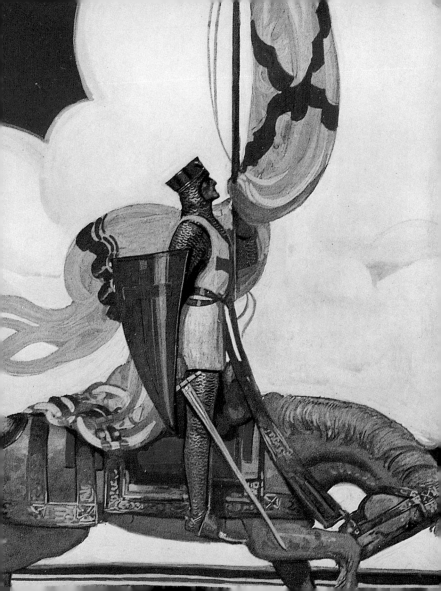

To the Cambro-Britons and Their Harp, his Ballad of Agincourt

FAIR stood the wind for France,
When we our sails advance,
Nor now to prove our chance,
Longer will tarry;
But putting to the main
At Kaux, the mouth of Seine,
With all his martial train,
Landed King Harry.
And taking many a fort,
Furnished in warlike sort,
Marcheth towards Agincourt,
In happy hour;
Skirmishing day by day
With those that stopped his way,
Where the French gen'ral lay
With all his power.
Which in his height of pride,
King Henry to deride,
His ransom to provide
To the King sending;
Which he neglects the while
As from the nation vile,
Yet with an angry smile
Their fall portending.
And turning to his men,
Quoth our brave Henry then:
Though they to one be ten,
Be not amazèd.

Yet have we well begun,
Battles so bravely won
Have ever to the sun
By fame been raisëd.
And for myself, quoth he,
This my full rest shall be,
England ne'er mourn for me,
Nor more esteem me;
Victor I will remain
Or on this earth lie slain,
Never shall she sustain
Loss to redeem me.
Poitiers and Crécy tell,
When most their pride did swell,
Under our swords they fell;
No less our skill is
Than when our grandsire great,
Claiming the regal seat
By many a warlike feat,
Lopped the French lilies.
The Duke of York so dread
The eager vaward led;
With the main Henry sped
Amongst his henchmen.
Excester had the rear,
A braver man not there,
O Lord, how hot they were
On the false Frenchmen!
They now to fight are gone,
Armor on armor shone,
Drum now to drum did groan,

To hear was wonder,
That with cries they make
The very earth did shake,
Trumpet to trumpet spake,
Thunder to thunder.
Well it thine age became,
O noble Erpingham,
Which didst the signal aim
To our hid forces;
When from a meadow by,
Like a storm suddenly,
The English archery
Stuck the French horses.
With Spanish yew so strong,
Arrows a cloth-yard long,
That like to serpents stung,
Piercing the weather;
None from his fellow starts,
But playing manly parts,
And like true English hearts,
Stuck close together.
When down their bows they threw,
And forth their bilboes drew,
And on the French they flew,
Not one was tardy;
Arms were from shoulders sent,
Scalps to the teeth were rent,
Down the French peasants went;
Our men were hardy.
This while our noble King,
His broad sword brandishing,

Down the French host did ding,
As to o'erwhelm it;
And many a deep wound lent,
His arms with blood besprent,
And many a cruel dent
Bruised his helmet.
Gloster, that Duke so good,
Next of the royal blood,
For famous England stood
With his brave brother;
Clarence, in steel so bright,
Though but a maiden knight,
Yet in that furious fight,
Scarce such another.
Warwick in blood did wade,
Oxford the foe invade,
And cruel slaughter made,
Still as they ran up;
Suffolk his ax did ply,
Beaumont and Willoughby
Bare them right doughtily,
Ferrers and Fanhope.
Upon Saint Crispin's day
Fought was this noble fray,
Which fame did not delay
To England to carry;
Oh, when shall English men
With such acts fill a pen,
Or England breed again
Such a King Harry?

Michael Drayton (1562–1631)

 95

Battle of the Baltic

Of Nelson and the North
Sing the glorious day's renown,
When to battle fierce came forth
All the might of Denmark's crown,
And her arms along the deep proudly shone;
By each gun the lighted brand
In a bold determined hand,
And the Prince of all the land
Led them on.

Like leviathans afloat
Lay their bulwarks on the brine,
While the sign of battle flew
On the lofty British line:
It was ten of April morn by the chime:
As they drifted on their path
There was silence deep as death,
And the boldest held his breath
For a time.

But the might of England flush'd
To anticipate the scene;
And her van the fleeter rush'd
O'er the deadly space between:
'Hearts of oak!' our captains cried, when each gun
From its adamantine lips
Spread a death-shade round the ships,
Like the hurricane eclipse
Of the sun.

Again! again! again!
And the havoc did not slack,
Till a feeble cheer the Dane
To our cheering sent us back;—
Their shots along the deep slowly boom:—
Then ceased—and all is wail,
As they strike the shatter'd sail,
Or in conflagration pale
Light the gloom.

Out spoke the victor then
As he hail'd them o'er the wave:
'Ye are brothers! ye are men!
And we conquer but to save:—
So peace instead of death let us bring:
But yield, proud foe, thy fleet,
With the crews, at England's feet,
And make submission meet
To our King.'...

Now joy, old England, raise!
For the tidings of thy might,
By the festal cities' blaze,
Whilst the wine-cup shines in light!
And yet amidst that joy and uproar,
Let us think of them that sleep
Full many a fathom deep,
By thy wild and stormy steep,
Elsinore!

Brave hearts! to Britain's pride
Once so faithful and so true,
On the deck of fame that died,
With the gallant, good Riou –
Soft sigh the winds of heaven o'er their grave!
While the billow mournful rolls,
And the mermaid's song condoles,
Singing glory to the souls
Of the brave!

Thomas Campbell (1777–1844)

The Due of the Dead

I sit beside my peaceful hearth,
With curtains drawn and lamp trimmed bright
I watch my children's noisy mirth;
I drink in home, and its delight.

I sip my tea, and criticise
The war, from flying rumours caught;
Trace on the map, to curious eyes,
How here they marched, and there they fought.

In intervals of household chat,
I lay down strategic laws
Why this manoeuvre, and why that;
Shape the event, or show the cause.

Or, in smooth dinner-table phrase,
'Twixt soup and fish, discuss the fight;
Give to each chief his blame or praise;
Say who was wrong and who was right.

Meanwhile o'er Alma's bloody plain
The scathe of battle has rolled by—
The wounded writhe and groan—the slain
Lie naked staring to the sky.

He out-worn surgeon plies his knife,
Nor pauses with the closing day;
While those who have escaped with life
Find food and fuel as they may.

And when their eyes in sleep they close,
After scant rations duly shared,
Plague picks his victims out, from those
Whom chance of battle may have spared.

Still when the bugle sounds the march,
He tracks his prey through steppe and dell;
Hangs fruit to tempt the throats that parch,
And poisens every stream and well.

All this with gallant hearts is done;
All this with patient hearts is borne:
And they by whom the laurel's won
Are seldom they by whom 'tis worn.

No deed, no suffering of the war,
But wins us fame, or spares us ill;
Those noble swords, though drawn afar,
Are guarding English homesteads still.

Owe we a debt to these brave men,
Unpaid by aught that's said or sung;
By leaders from a ready pen,
Or phrases from a flippant tongue.

The living, England's hand my crown
With Recognition, frank and free;
With titles, medals, and renown;
The wounded shall our pensioners be.

But they, who meet a soldier's doom–
Think you, it is enough, good friend,
To plant the laurel at their tomb,
And carve their names–and there an end?

No. They are gone: but there are left
Those they loved best while they were here–
Parents made childless, babes bereft,
Desolate widows, sisters dear.

All these let grateful England take;
And, with a large and liberal heart,
Cherish, for her slain soldiers' sake,
And of her fullness give them part.

Fold them within her sheltering breast;
Their parent, husband, brother, prove.
That so the dead may be at rest,
Knowing those cared for whom they love.

William Makepeace Thackeray (1811–63)

Bivouac on a Mountain Side

I SEE before me now, a traveling army halting;
Below, a fertile valley spread, with barns, and the orchards of summer;
Behind, the terraced sides of a mountain, abrupt in places, rising high;
Broken, with rocks, with clinging cedars, with tall shapes, dingily seen;
The numerous camp-fires scatter'd near and far, some away up on
   the mountain;
The shadowy forms of men and horses, looming,
large-sized flickering;
And over all, the sky—the sky! far, far out of reach,
   studded, breaking out, the eternal stars.

Walt Whitman (1819–92)

The Bivouac In The Snow

Halt! – the march is over,
Day is almost done;
Loose the cumbrous knapsack,
Drop the heavy gun.
Chilled and wet and weary,
Wander to and fro,
Seeking wood to kindle
Fires amidst the snow.

Round the bright blaze gather,
Heed not sleet or cold;
Ye are Spartan soldiers,
Stout and brave and bold.
Never Xerxian army
Yet subdued a foe
Who but asked a blanket
On a bed of snow.

Shivering, 'midst the darkness,
Christian men are found,
There devoutly kneeling
On the frozen ground –
Pleading for their country,
In its hour of woe –
For the soldiers marching
Shoeless through the snow.

Lost in heavy slumbers,
Free from toil and strife,
Dreaming of their dear ones
Home, and child, and wife –
Tentless they are lying,
While the fires burn low –
Lying in their blankets
'Midst December's snow.

Margaret Junkin Preston (1820–97)

Good-Night In War-Time

The stars we saw arise are high above,
And yet our Evensong seems sung too soon.
Good-Night! I lay my hand–with such a love
As thou wert brother of my blood–upon
Thy shoulder, and methinks beneath the moon
Those sisters, Anglia and Caledon,
Lean towards each other. Aye, for Man is one;
We are a host ruled by one trumpet-call,
Where each, armed in his sort, makes as he may
The general motion. The well-tuned array
We see; yet to what victory in what wars
We see not; but like the revolving stars
Move on ourselves. The total march of all
Or men or stars God knows. Lord, lead us on!

Sydney Thompson Dobell (1824–74)

Home, In War-Time

She turned the fair page with her fairer hand–
More fair and frail than it was wont to be–
O'er each remembered thing he loved to see
She lingered, and as with a fairy's wand
Enchanted it to order. Oft she fanned
New motes into the sun; and as a bee
Sings thro' a brake of bells, so murmured she,
And so her patient love did understand
The reliquary room. Upon the sill
She fed his favourite bird. 'Ah, Robin, sing!
He loves thee.' Then she touches a sweet string
Of soft recall, and towards the Eastern hill
Smiles all her soul–for him who cannot hear
The raven croaking at his carrion ear.

Sydney Thompson Dobell (1824–74)

The Army Surgeon

Over that breathing waste of friends and foes,
The wounded and the dying, hour by hour,-
In will a thousand, yet but one in power,-
He labours thro' the red and groaning day.
The fearful moorland where the myriads lay
Moved as a moving field of mangled worms.
And as a raw brood, orphaned in the storms,
Thrust up their heads if the wind bend a spray
Above them, but when the bare branch performs
No sweet parental office, sink away
With hopeless chirp of woe, so as he goes
Around his feet in clamorous agony
They rise and fall; and all the seething plain
Bubbles a cauldron vast of many-coloured pain.

Sydney Thompson Dobell (1824–74)

The Picket Guard

"ALL quiet along the Potomac to-night!"
Except here and there a stray picket
Is shot, as he walks on his beat, to and fro,
By a rifleman hid in the thicket.
'Tis nothing! a private or two now and then
Will not count in the news of a battle;
Not an officer lost, only one of the men
Moaning out, all alone, the death rattle.
All quiet along the Potomac to-night!
Where the soldiers lie peacefully dreaming;
And their tents in the rays of the clear autumn moon,
And the light of their camp-fires are gleaming.
A tremulous sigh, as a gentle night-wind
Through the forest leaves slowly is creeping;
While the stars up above, with their glittering eyes,
Keep guard o'er the army sleeping.
There's only the sound of the lone sentry's tread
As he tramps from the rock to the fountain,
And thinks of the two on the low trundel bed,
Far away, in the cot on the mountain.
His musket falls slack, his face, dark and grim,
Grows gentle with memories tender,
As he mutters a prayer for the children asleep,
And their mother–"may heaven defend her!"
The moon seems to shine forth as brightly as then–
That night, when the love, yet unspoken,
Leaped up to his lips, and when low-murmured vows
Were pledged to be ever unbroken.
Then drawing his sleeve roughly over his eyes,

He dashes off tears that are welling;
And gathers the gun closer up to his breast
As if to keep down his heart's swelling.
He passes the fountain, the blasted pine-tree,
And his footstep is lagging and weary;
Yet onward he goes, through the broad belt of light,
Towards the shades of the forest so dreary.
Hark! was it the night-wind that rustled the leaves?
Was it the moonlight so wondrously flashing?
It looked like a rifle: "Ha! Mary, good-by!"
And his life-blood is ebbing and plashing.
"All quiet along the Potomac to-night!"
No sound save the rush of the river;
While soft falls the dew on the face of the dead,
And the picket's off duty forever!

Ethyl Lynn Beers (1827–79)

The Guards Came Through

MEN of the Twenty-first
Up by the Chalk Pit Wood,
Weak with our wounds and our thirst,
Wanting our sleep and our food,
After a day and a night –
God, shall we ever forget!
Beaten and broke in the fight,
But sticking it – sticking it yet.
Trying to hold the line,
Fainting and spent and done,
Always the thud and the whine,
Always the yell of the Hun!
Northumerland, Lancaster, York,
Durham and Somerset,
Fighting alone, worn to the bone,
But sticking it – sticking it yet.
Never a message of hope!
Never a word of cheer!
Fronting Hill 70's shell-swept slope,
With the dull dead plain in our rear.
Always the whine of the shell,
Always the roar of its burst,
Always the tortures of hell,
As waiting and wincing we cursed
Our luck and the guns and the Boche,
When our Corporal shouted, "Stand to!"
And I heard some one cry, "Clear the front for the Guards!"
And the Guards came through.
Our throats they were parched and hot,

But Lord, if you'd heard the cheers!
Irish and Welsh and Scot,
Coldstream and Grenadiers.
Two brigades, if you please,
Dressing as straight as a hem,
We – we were down on our knees,
Praying for us and for them!
Lord, I could speak for a week,
But how could you understand!
How should your cheeks be wet,
Such feelin's don't come to you.
But when can me or my mates forget,
When the Guards came through?
"Five yards left extend!"
It passed from rank to rank.
Line after line with never a bend,
And a touch of the London swank.
A trifle of swank and dash,
Cool as a home parade,
Twinkle and glitter and flash,
Flinching never a shade,
With the shrapnel right in their face
Doing their Hyde Park stunt,
Keeping their swing at an easy pace,
Arms at the trail, eyes front!
Man, it was great to see!
Man, it was fine to do!
It's a cot and a hospital ward for me,
But I'll tell'em in Blighty, whereever I be,
How the Guards came through.

Arthur Conan Doyle (1859–1930)

 117

The Anxious Dead

O guns, fall silent till the dead men hear
Above their heads the legions pressing on:
(These fought their fight in time of bitter fear,
And died not knowing how the day had gone.)

O flashing muzzles, pause, and let them see
The coming dawn that streaks the sky afar;
Then let your mighty chorus witness be
To them, and Caesar, that we still make war.

Tell them, O guns, that we have heard their call,
That we have sworn, and will not turn aside,
That we will onward till we win or fall,
That we will keep the faith for which they died.

Bid them be patient, and some day, anon,
They shall feel earth enwrapt in silence deep;
Shall greet, in wonderment, the quiet dawn,
And in content may turn them to their sleep.

John McCrae (1872–1918)

War

A tent that is pitched at the base:
A wagon that comes from the night:
A stretcher-and on it a Case:
A surgeon, who's holding a light. The Infantry's bearing
  the brunt –
O hark to the wind-carried cheer! A mutter of guns at the
  front:
A whimper of sobs at the rear.
And it's War! 'Orderly, hold the light.
You can lay him down on the table: so. Easily-gently!
Thanks – you may go.'
And it's War! but the part that is not for show.

II

A tent, with a table athwart,
A table that's laid out for one;
A waterproof cover-and nought
But the limp, mangled work of a gun.
A bottle that's stuck by the pole
A guttering dip in its neck; The flickering light of a soul
On the wondering eyes of The Wreck, And it's War!
'Orderly, hold his hand.
I'm not going to hurt you, so don't be afraid.
A ricochet! God! what a mess it has made!'
And it's War! and a very unhealthy trade.

III

The clink of a stopper and glass:
A sigh as the chloroform drips:
A trickle of-what? on the grass, And bluer and bluer the lips.
The lashes have hidden the stare ...
A rent, and the clothes fall away ...
A touch, and the wound is laid bare ...
A cut, and the face has turned grey ...
And it's War! 'Orderly, take It out.
It's hard for his child, and it's rough on his wife,
There might have been-sooner-a chance for his life.
But it's War! And-Orderly, clean this knife!'

Edgar Wallace (1875–1932)

Grotesque

These are the damned circles Dante trod,
Terrible in hopelessness,
But even skulls have their humor,
An eyeless and sardonic mockery:
And we,
Sitting with streaming eyes in the acrid smoke,
That murks our foul, damp billet,
Chant bitterly, with raucous voices
As a choir of frogs
In hideous irony, our patriotic songs.

Frederic Manning (1882–1935)

The Trenches

Endless lanes sunken in the clay,
Bays, and traverses, fringed with wasted herbage,
Seed-pods of blue scabious, and some lingering blooms;
And the sky, seen as from a well,
Brilliant with frosty stars.
We stumble, cursing, on the slippery duck-boards.
Goaded like the damned by some invisible wrath,
A will stronger than weariness, stronger than animal fear,
Implacable and monotonous.

Here a shaft, slanting, and below
A dusty and flickering light from one feeble candle
And prone figures sleeping uneasily,
Murmuring,
And men who cannot sleep,
With faces impassive as masks,
Bright, feverish eyes, and drawn lips,
Sad, pitiless, terrible faces,
Each an incarnate curse.

Here in a bay, a helmeted sentry
Silent and motionless, watching while two sleep,
And he sees before him
With indifferent eyes the blasted and torn land
Peopled with stiff prone forms, stupidly rigid,
As tho' they had not been men.

Dead are the lips where love laughed or sang,
The hands of youth eager to lay hold of life,
Eyes that have laughed to eyes,
And these were begotten,
O Love, and lived lightly, and burnt
With the lust of a man's first strength: ere they were rent,
Almost at unawares, savagely; and strewn
In bloody fragments, to be the carrion
Of rats and crows.

And the sentry moves not, searching
Night for menace with weary eyes.

Frederic Manning (1882–1935)

Woodbine Willie

They gave me this name like their nature,
Compacted of laughter and tears,
A sweet that was born of the bitter,
A joke that was torn from the years
Of their travail and torture, Christ's fools,
Atoning my sins with their blood,
Who grinned in their agony sharing
The glorious madness of God.
Their name! Let me hear it – the symbol
Of unpaid – unpayable debt,
For the men to whom I owed God's Peace,
I put off with a cigarette.

G. A. Studdart Kennedy (1883–1929)

Break of Day in the Trenches

The darkness crumbles away.
It is the same old druid Time as ever,
Only a live ting leaps my hand,
A qweer sardonic rat,
As I pull the parapet's poppy
To stick behind my ear.
Droll rat, they would shoot you if they knew
Your cosmopolitan sympathies.
Now you have touched this English hand
You will do the same to a German
Soon, no doubt, if it be your pleasure
To cross the sleeping green between.
It seems you inwardly grin as you pass
Strong eyes, fine limbs, haughty athletes,
Less chanced than you for life,
Bonds to the whims of murder,
Sprawled in the bowels of the earth,
The torn fields of France.
What do you see in our eyes
At the shrieking iron and flame
Hurled through the still heavens?
What quaver—what hear aghast?
Poppies whose roots are in man's veins
Drop, and are every dropping;
But mine in my ear is safe—
Just a little white with the dust.

Isaac Rosenberg (1890–1918)

Returning, We Hear the Larks

Sombre the night is.
And though we have our lives, we know
What sinister threat lurks there.

Dragging these anguished limbs, we only know
This poison-blasted track opens on our camp–
On a little safe sleep.

But hark! joy–joy–strange joy.
Lo! heights of night ringing with unseen larks.
Music showering our upturned list'ning faces.

Death could not drop from the dark
As easily as song–
But song only dropped,
Like a blind man's dreams on the sand
By dangerous tides,
Like a girl's dark hair for she dreams no ruin lies there,
Or her kisses where a serpent hides.

Isaac Rosenberg (1890–1918)

Louse Hunting

Nudes – stark and glistening,
Yelling in lurid glee. Grinning faces
And raging limbs
Whirl over the floor one fire.
For a shirt verminously busy
Yon soldier tore from his throat, with oaths
Godhead might shrink at, but not the lice.
And soon the shirt was aflare
Over the candle he'd lit while we lay.
Then we all sprang up and stript
To hunt the verminous brood.
Soon like a demons' pantomine
The place was raging.
See the silhouettes agape,
See the glibbering shadows
Mixed with the battled arms on the wall.
See gargantuan hooked fingers
Pluck in supreme flesh
To smutch supreme littleness.
See the merry limbs in hot Highland fling
Because some wizard vermin
Charmed from the quiet this revel
When our ears were half lulled
By the dark music
Blown from Sleep's trumpet.

Isaac Rosenberg (1890–1918)

In Memoriam Private D. Sutherland killed in Action in the German Trench, May 16, 1916, and the Others who Died

So you were David's father,
And he was your only son,
And the new-cut peats are rotting
And the work is left undone,
Because of an old man weeping,
Just an old man in pain,
For David, his son David,
That will not come again.

Oh, the letters he wrote you,
And I can see them still,
Not a word of the fighting
But just the sheep on the hill
And how you should get the crops in
Ere the year got stormier,
And the Bosches have got his body,
And I was his officer.

You were only David's father,
But I had fifty sons
When we went up in the evening
Under the arch of the guns,
And we came back at twilight –
O God! I heard them call
To me for help and pity
That could not help at all.

Oh, never will I forget you,
My men that trusted me,
More my sons than your fathers',
For they could only see
The little helpless babies
And the young men in their pride.
They could not see you dying,
And hold you while you died.

Happy and young and gallant,
They saw their first-born go,
But not the strong limbs broken
And the beautiful men brought low,
The piteous writhing bodies,
They screamed, 'Don't leave me, Sir,'
For they were only your fathers
But I was your officer.

E. A. Mackintosh (1893–1917)

Futility

Move him into the sun—
Gently its touch awoke him once,
At home, whispering of fields unsown.
Always it woke him, even in France,
Until this morning, and this snow.
If anything might rouse him now
The kind old sun will know.
Think how it wakes the seeds—
Woke, once, the clays of a cold star.
Are limbs, so dear-achieved, are sides,
Full-nerved—still warm—too hard to stir?
Was it for this the clay grew tall?
—O what made fatuous sunbeams toil
To break the earth's sleep at all?

Wilfred Owen (1893–1918)

Exposure

I

Our brains ache, in the merciless iced east winds that knife us...
Wearied we keep awake because the night is silent...
Low drooping flares confuse our memory of the salient...
Worried by silence, sentries whisper, curious, nervous,
But nothing happens.

Watching, we hear the mad gusts tugging on the wire.
Like twitching agonies of men among its brambles.
Northward incessantly, the flickering gunnery rumbles,
Far off, like a dull rumour of some other war.
What are we doing here?

The poignant misery of dawn begins to grow...
We only know war lasts, rain soaks, and clouds sag stormy.
Dawn massing in the east her melancholy army
Attacks once more in ranks on shivering ranks of gray,
But nothing happens.

Sudden successive flights of bullets streak the silence.
Less deadly than the air that shudders black with snow,
With sidelong flowing flakes that flock, pause and renew,
We watch them wandering up and down the wind's nonchalance,
But nothing happens.

II

Pale flakes with lingering stealth come feeling for our faces –
We cringe in holes, back on forgotten dreams, and stare, snow-dazed,
Deep into grassier ditches. So we drowse, sun-dozed,
Littered with blossoms trickling where the blackbird fusses.
Is it that we are dying?

Slowly our ghosts drag home: glimpsing the sunk fires glozed
With crusted dark-red jewels; crickets jingle there;
For hours the innocent mice rejoice: the house is theirs;
Shutters and doors all closed: on us the doors are closed –
We turn back to our dying.

Since we believe not otherwise can kind fires burn;
Now ever suns smile true on child, or field, or fruit.
For God's invincible spring our love is made afraid;
Therefore, not loath, we lie out here; therefore were born,
For love of God seems dying.

To-night, His frost will fasten on this mud and us,
Shrivelling many hands and puckering foreheads crisp.
The burying-party, picks and shovels in their shaking grasp,
Pause over half-known faces. All their eyes are ice,
But nothing happens.

Wilfred Owen (1893–1918)

Apologia pro Poemate Meo

I, too, saw God through mud, –
The mud that cracked on cheeks when wretches smiled.
War brought more glory to their eyes than blood,
And gave their laughs more glee than shakes a child.

Merry it was to laugh there –
Where death becomes absurd and life absurder.
For power was on us as we slashed bones bare
Not to feel sickness or remorse of murder.

I, too, have dropped off Fear –
Behind the barrage, dead as my platoon,
And sailed my spirit surging light and clear
Past the entanglement where hopes lay strewn;

'And witnessed exultation –
Faces that used to curse me, scowl for scowl,
Shine and lift up with passion of oblation,
Seraphic for an hour; though they were foul.

I have made fellowships –
Untold of happy lovers in old song.
For love is not the binding of fair lips
With the soft silk of eyes that look and long,

By Joy, whose ribbon slips, –
But wound with war's hard wire whose stakes are strong;
Bound with the bandage of the arm that drips;
Knit in the webbing of the rifle-thong.

I have perceived much beauty
In the hoarse oaths that kept our courage straight;
Heard music in the silentness of duty;
Found peace where shell-storms spouted reddest spate.

Nevertheless, except you share
With them in hell the sorrowful dark of hell,
Whose world is but the trembling of a flare
And heaven but as the highway for a shell,

You shall not hear their mirth:
You shall not come to think them well content
By any jest of mine. These men are worth
Your tears. You are not worth their merriment.

Wilfred Owen (1893–1918)

Greater Love

Red lips are not so red
As the stained stones kissed by the English dead.
Kindness of wooed and wooer
Seems shame to their love pure.
O Love, your eyes lose lure
When I behold eyes blinded in my stead!

Your slender attitude
Trembles not exquisite like limbs knife-skewed,
Rolling and rolling there
Where God seems not to care:
Till the fierce love they bear
Cramps them in death's extreme decrepitude.

Your voice sings not so soft, —
Though even as wind murmuring through raftered loft, —
Your dear voice is not dear,
Gentle, and evening clear,
As theirs whom none now hear,
Now earth has stopped their piteous mouths that coughed.

Heart, you were never hot
Nor large, nor full like hearts made great with shot;
And though your hand be pale,
Paler are all which trail
Your cross through flame and hail:
Weep, you may weep, for you may touch them not.

Wilfred Owen (1893–1918)

THE HARSH REALITIES OF WAR

The Lament of Maev Leith-Dherg

Raise the Cromlech high!
  MacMoghcorb is slain,
And other men's renown
  Has to live again.

Cold at last he lies
  Neath the burial-stone;
All the blood he shed
  Could not save his own.

Stately-strong he went,
  Through his nobles all
When we paced together
  Up the banquet-hall.

Dazzling white as lime
  Was his body fair,
Cherry-red his cheeks,
  Raven-black his hair.

Razor-sharp his spear,
  And the shield he bore,
High as champion's head–
  His arm was like an oar.

Never aught but truth
  Spake my noble king;
Valour all his trust
  In all his warfaring.

As the forked pole
  Holds the roof-tree's weight,
So my hero's arm
  Held the battle straight.

Terror went before him,
  Death behind his back;
Well the wolves of Erinn
  Knew his chariot's track.

Seven bloody battles
  He broke upon his foes;
In each a hundred heroes
  Fell beneath his blows.

Once he fought at Fossud
  Thrice at Ath-finn-Fail
'Twas my king that conquered
  At bloody Ath-and-Scail.

At the boundary Stream
  Fought the Royal Hound,
And for Bernas Battle
  Stands his name renowned.

Here he fought with Leinster–
  Last of all his frays–
On the hill of Cucorb's Fate
  High his Cromlech raise.

Anonymous (11th Century)

 147

Extract from Astrophel

Such skill matcht with such courage as he had,
Did prick him foorth with proud desire of praise:
To seek abroad, of daunger nought y'drad,
His mistresse name, and his owne fame to raise.
What need[eth] perill to be sought abroad,
Since round about vs, it doth make aboad?
It fortuned as he, that perlous game
In forreine soyle pursued far away:
Into a forest wide, and waste he came
Where store he heard to be of saluage pray.
So wide a forest and so waste as this,
Nor famous Ardeyn, nor fowle Arlo is.
There his welwouen toyles and subtil traines,
He laid the brutish nation to enwrap:
So well he wrought with practise and with paines,
That he of them great troups did soone entrap.
Full happie man (misweening much) was hee,
So rich a spoile within his power to see.
Eftsoones all heedlesse of his dearest hale,
Full greedily into the heard he thrust:
To slaughter them, and work their finall bale,
Least that his tolye should of their troups be brust.
Wide wounds emongst them many a one he made,
Now with his sharp borespeare, now with his blade.
His care was all how he them all might kill,
That none might scape (so partiall vnto none)
Ill mynd so much to mynd anothers ill,
As to become vnmyndfull of his owne.
But pardon that vnto the cruell skies,

That from himselfe to them withdrew his eies.
So as he rag'd emongst that beastly rout,
A cruell beast of most accursed brood:
Vpon him turnd (despeyre makes cowards stout)
And with fell tooth accustomed to blood,
Launched his thigh with so mischieuous might,
That it both bone and muscles ryued quight.
So deadly was the dint and deep the wound,
And so huge streames of blood thereout did flow:
That he endured not the direfull stound,
But on the cold deare earth himselfe did throw.
The whiles the captiue heard his nets did rend,
And hauing none to let, to wood did wend.
Ah where were ye this while his shepheard peares,
To whom aliue was nought so deare as hee:
And ye faire Mayds the matches of his yeares,
Which in his grace did boast you most to bee?
Ah where were ye, when he of you had need,
To stop his wound that wondrously did bleed?
Ah wretched boy the shape of dreryhead,
And sad ensample of mans suddein end:
Full litle faileth but thou shalt be dead,
Vnpitied, vnplaynd, of foe or frend.
Whilest none is nigh, thine eylids vp to close,
And kisse thy lips like faded leaues of rose.

Edmund Spenser (1552–99)

A Burnt Ship

Out of a fired ship, which by no way
But drowning could be rescued from the flame,
Some men leap'd forth, and ever as they came
Near the foes' ships, did by their shot decay;
So all were lost, which in the ship were found,
They in the sea being burnt, they in the burnt ship drown'd.

John Donne (1572–1631)

Extract from Paradise Lost

They ended parle, and both addressed for fight
Unspeakable; for who, though with the tongue
Of Angels, can relate, or to what things
Liken on earth conspicuous, that may lift
Human imagination to such highth
Of Godlike power? for likest Gods they seemed,
Stood they or moved, in stature, motion, arms,
Fit to decide the empire of great Heaven.
Now waved their fiery swords, and in the air
Made horrid circles; two broad suns their shields
Blazed opposite, while Expectation stood
In horrour: From each hand with speed retired,
Where erst was thickest fight, the angelick throng,
And left large field, unsafe within the wind
Of such commotion; such as, to set forth
Great things by small, if, nature's concord broke,
Among the constellations war were sprung,
Two planets, rushing from aspect malign
Of fiercest opposition, in mid sky
Should combat, and their jarring spheres confound.
Together both with next to almighty arm
Up-lifted imminent, one stroke they aimed
That might determine, and not need repeat,
As not of power at once; nor odds appeared
In might or swift prevention: But the sword
Of Michael from the armoury of God
Was given him tempered so, that neither keen
Nor solid might resist that edge: it met
The sword of Satan, with steep force to smite

Descending, and in half cut sheer; nor staid,
But with swift wheel reverse, deep entering, shared
All his right side: Then Satan first knew pain,
And writhed him to and fro convolved; so sore
The griding sword with discontinuous wound
Passed through him: But the ethereal substance closed,
Not long divisible; and from the gash
A stream of necturous humour issuing flowed
Sanguine, such as celestial Spirits may bleed,
And all his armour stained, ere while so bright.
Forthwith on all sides to his aid was run
By Angels many and strong, who interposed
Defence, while others bore him on their shields
Back to his chariot, where it stood retired
From off the files of war: There they him laid
Gnashing for anguish, and despite, and shame,
To find himself not matchless, and his pride
Humbled by such rebuke, so far beneath
His confidence to equal God in power.
Yet soon he healed; for Spirits that live throughout
Vital in every part, not as frail man
In entrails, heart of head, liver or reins,
Cannot but by annihilating die;
Nor in their liquid texture mortal wound
Receive, no more than can the fluid air:
All heart they live, all head, all eye, all ear,
All intellect, all sense; and, as they please,
They limb themselves, and colour, shape, or size
Assume, as?kikes them best, condense or rare.

John Milton (1608–74)

✕ 157 ✕

On the late Massacre in Piedmont

Avenge, O Lord, thy slaughtered saints, whose bones
  Lie scattered on the Alpine mountains cold,
  Even them who kept thy truth so pure of old
  When all our fathers worshipped stocks and stones,
Forget no; in thy book record their groans
  Who were thy sheep and in their ancient fold
  Slain by the bloody Piedmontese that rolled

Mother with infant down the rocks. Their moans
The vales redoubled to the hills, and they
To Heaven. Their martyred blood and ashes sow
O'er all th' Italian fields where still doth sway
The triple tyrant, that from these may grow
A hundredfold, who having learnt thy way,
Early may fly the Babylonian woe.

John Milton (1608–74)

War

O War, What art thou?
After the brightest conquest, what remains
Of all thy glories? For the vanquish'd – chains –
For the proud victor – what? Alas! to reign
O'er desolated nations – a drear waste,
By one man's crime, by one man's lust of power,
Unpeopled! Naked plains and ravaged fields,
Succeed to smiling harvests and the fruits
Of peaceful olive – luscious fig and vine!
Here, rifled temples are the cavern'd dens
Of savage beasts, or haunt of birds obscene;
There, populous cities blacken in the sun,
And in the general wreck proud palaces
Lie undistinguish'd, save by the dun smoke
Of recent conflagration! When the song
Of dear-bought joy, with many a triumph swell'd,
Salutes the victory's ear, and soothes his pride,
How is the grateful harmony profaned
With the sad dissonance of virgins' cries,
Who mourn their brothers slain! Of matrons hoar,
Who clasp their wither'd hands, and fondly ask
With iteration shrill – their slaughter'd sons!
How is the laurel's verdure stain'd with blood
And soil'd with widows' tears!

Hannah More (1745–1833)

Extract from the Vision of Don Roderick

From a rude isle, his ruder lineage came.
  The spark, that, from a suburb hovel's hearth
Ascending, wraps some capital in flame,
  Hath not a meaner or more sordid birth.
And for the soul that bade him waste the earth—
  The sable land-flood from some swamp obscure,
That poisons the glad husband-field with dearth,
  And by destruction bids its fame endure,
Hath not a source more sullen, stagnant, and impure.

Before that Leader strode a shadowy form,
  Her limbs like mist, her torch like meteor shew'd;
With which she beckon'd him through fight and storm,
  And all he crush'd that cross'd his desp'rate road,
Nor thought, nor fear'd, nor look'd on what he trode;
  Realms could not glut his pride, blood not slake,
So oft as e'er she shook her torch abroad—
  It was Ambition bade his terrors wake;
Nor deign'd she, as of yore, a milder form to take.

No longer now she spurn'd at mean revenge,
  Or stay'd her hand for conquer'd freeman's moan,
As when, the fates of aged Rome to change,
  By Caesar's side she cross'd the Rubicon;
Nor joy'd she to bestow the spoils she won,
  As when the banded Powers of Greece were task'd
To war beneath the Youth of Macedon:
  No seemly veil her modern minion ask'd,
He saw her hideous face, and lov'd the fiend unmask'd.

That Prelate mark'd his march — On banners blaz'd
  With battles won in many a distant land.
On eagle standards and on arms he gaz'd;
  "And hop'st thou, then," he said, "thy power shall stand?
O! thou hast builded on the shifting sand,
  And thou hast temper'd it with slaughter's flood;
And know, fell scourge in the Almighty's hand,
  Gore-moisten'd trees shall perish in the bud,
And, by a bloody death, shall die the Man of Blood."

The ruthless Leader beckon'd from his train
  A wan, paternal shade, and bade him kneel,
And pale his temples with the Crown of Spain,
  While trumpets rang, and Heralds cried, "Castile!"
Not that he lov'd him — No! — in no man's weal,
  Scarce in his own, e'er joy'd that sullen heart;
Yet round that throne he bade his warriors wheel,
  That the poor puppet might perform his part,
And be a scepter'd slave, at his stern beck to start.

Walter Scott (1771–1832)

Extract from Fears in Solitude

It weighs upon the heart, that he must think
What uproar and what strife may now be stirring
This way or that way o'er these silent hills–
Invasion, and the thunder and the shout,
And all the crash of onset; fear and rage,
And undetermined conflict–even now,
Even now, perchance, and in his native isle:
Carnage and groans beneath this blessed sun!
We have offended, Oh! my countrymen!
We have offended very grievously,
And been most tyrannous. From east to west
A groan of accusation pierces Heaven!
The wretched plead against us; multitudes
Countless and vehement, the sons of God,
Our brethren! Like a cloud that travels on,
Steamed up from Cairo's swamps of pestilence,
Even so, my countrymen! have we gone forth
And borne to distant tribes slavery and pangs,
And, deadlier far, our vices, whose deep taint
With slow perdition murders the whole man,
His body and his soul! Meanwhile, at home,
All individual dignity and power
Engulfed in Courts, Committees, Institutions,
Associations and Societies,
A vain, speach-mouthing, speech-reporting Guild,
One Benefit-Club for mutual flattery,
We have drunk up, demure as at a grace,
Pollutions from the brimming cup of wealth;
Contemptuous of all honourable rule,

Yet bartering freedom and the poor man's life
For gold, as at a market! The sweet words
Of Christian promise, words that even yet
Might stem destruction, were they wisely preached,
Are muttered o'er by men, whose tones proclaim
How flat and wearisome they feel their trade:
Rank scoffers some, but most too indolent
To deem them falsehoods or to know their truth.
Oh! blasphemous! the Book of Life is made
A superstitious instrument, on which
We gabble o'er the oaths we mean to break;

Samuel Taylor Coleridge (1772–1834)

The Charge of the Light Brigade

I

Half a league, half a league,
Half a league onward,
All in the valley of Death
Rode the six hundred.
'Forward, the Light Brigade!
Charge for the guns!' he said:
Into the valley of Death
Rode the six hundred.

II

'Forward, the Light Brigade!'
Was there a man dismay'd?
Not tho' the soldier knew
Some one had blunder'd:
Theirs not to make reply,
Theirs not to reason why,
Theirs but to do and die:
Into the valley of Death
Rode the six hundred.

III

Cannon to right of them,
Cannon to left of them,
Cannon in front of them
Volley'd and thunder'd;
Storm'd at with shot and shell,
Boldly they rode and well,
Into the jaws of Death,
Into the mouth of Hell
Rode the six hundred.

IV

Flash'd all their sabres bare,
Flash'd as they turn'd in air
Sabring the gunners there,
Charging an army, while
All the world wonder'd:
Plunged in the battery-smoke
Right thro' the line they broke;
Cossack and Russian
Reel'd from the sabre-stroke
Shatter'd and sunder'd.
Then they rode back, but not
Not the six hundred.

V

Cannon to right of them,
Cannon to left of them,
Cannon behind them
Volley'd and thunder'd;
Storm'd at with shot and shell,
While horse and hero fell,
They that had fought so well
Came thro' the jaws of Death,
Back from the mouth of Hell,
All that was left of them,
Left of six hundred.

VI

When can their glory fade?
O the wild charge they made!
All the world wonder'd.
Honour the charge they made!
Honour the Light Brigade,
Noble six hundred!

Alfred, Lord Tennyson (1809–92)

Shiloh - A Requiem

Skimming lightly, wheeling still,
The swallows fly low
Over the field in clouded days,
The forest-field of Shiloh –
Over the field where April rain
Solaced the parched one stretched in pain
Through the pause of night
That followed the Sunday fight
Around the church of Shiloh–
The church so lone, the log-built one,
That echoed to many a parting groan
And natural prayer
Of dying foemen mingled there –
Foemen at morn, but friends at eve –
Fame or country least their care:
(What like a bullet can undeceive!)
But now they lie low,
While over them the swallows skim,
And all is hushed at Shiloh.

Herman Melville (1819–91)

Come up from the Fields, Father

I

COME up from the fields, father, here's a letter from our Pete;
And come to the front door, mother—here's a letter from thy dear son.

II

Lo, 'tis autumn;
Lo, where the trees, deeper green, yellower and redder,
Cool and sweeten Ohio's villages, with leaves fluttering in the moderate wind;
Where apples ripe in the orchards hang, and grapes on the trellis'd vines;
(Smell you the smell of the grapes on the vines?
Smell you the buckwheat, where the bees were lately buzzing?)

Above all, lo, the sky, so calm, so transparent after the rain, and with
  wondrous cloud
Below, too, all calm, all vital and beautiful—and the farm prospers well.

III

Down in the fields all prospers well;
But now from the fields come, father—come at the daughter's call;
And come to the entry, mother—to the front door come, right away.

Fast as she can she hurries—something ominous—her steps trembling;
She does not tarry to smoothe her hair, nor adjust her cap.

Open the envelope quickly;
O this is not our son's writing, yet his name is sign'd;
O a strange hand writes for our dear son—O stricken mother's soul!
All swims before her eyes—flashes with black—she catches the main
  words only;
Sentences broken—*gun-shot wound in the breast, cavalry skirmish, taken to hospital,*
At present low, but will soon be better.

IV

Ah, now, the single figure to me,
Amid all teeming and wealthy Ohio, with all its cities and farms,
Sickly white in the face, and dull in the head, very faint,
By the jamb of a door leans.

Grieve not so, dear mother, (the just-grown daughter speaks through her sobs;
The little sisters huddle around, speechless and dismay'd;)
See, dearest mother, the letter says Pete will soon be better.

V

Alas, poor boy, he will never be better, (nor may-be needs to be better,
  that brave and simple soul;)
While they stand at home at the door, he is dead already;
The only son is dead.

But the mother needs to be better;
She, with thin form, presently drest in black;
By day her meals untouch'd—then at night fitfully sleeping, often waking,
In the midnight waking, weeping, longing with one deep longing,
O that she might withdraw unnoticed—silent from life, escape and withdraw
To follow, to seek, to be with her dear dead son.

Walt Whitman (1819–92)

Extract from Sohrab and Rustum

HE ceas'd, but while he spake, Rustum had risen,
And stood erect, trembling with rage; his club
He left to lie, but had regain'd his spear,
Whose fiery point now in his mail'd right-hand
Blaz'd bright and baleful, like that autumn-star,
The baleful sign of fevers; dust had soil'd
His stately crest, and dimm'd his glittering arms.
His breast heav'd, his lips foam'd, and twice his voice
Was chok'd with rage; at last these words broke way:—
  "Girl! nimble with thy feet, not with thy hands!
Curl'd minion, dancer, coiner of sweet words!
Fight, let me hear thy hateful voice no more!
Thou art not in Afrasiab's gardens now
With Tartar girls, with whom thou art wont to dance;
But on the Oxus-sands, and in the dance
Of battle, and with me, who make no play
Of war; I fight it out, and hand to hand.
Speak not to me of truce, and pledge, and wine!
Remember all thy valor; try thy feints
And cunning! all the pity I had is gone;
Because thou hast sham'd me before both the hosts
With thy light skipping tricks, and thy girl's wiles."
  He spoke, and Sohrab kindled at his taunts,
And he too drew his sword; at once they rush'd
Together as two eagles on one prey
Come rushing down together from the clouds,
One from the east, one from the west; their shields
Dash'd with a clang together, and a din
Rose, such as that the sinewy woodcutters

Make often in the forest's heart at morn,
Of hewing axes, crashing trees — such blows
Rustum and Sohrab on each other hail'd.
And you would say that sun and stars took part
In that unnatural conflict; for a cloud
Grew suddenly in Heaven, and dark'd the sun
Over the fighters' heads; and a wind rose
Under their feet, and moaning swept the plain,
And in a sandy whirlwind wrapp'd the pair.
In gloom they twain were wrapp'd, and they alone;
For both the on-looking hosts on either hand
Stood in broad daylight, and the sky was pure,
And the sun sparkled on the Oxus stream.
But in the gloom they fought, with blood-shot eyes
And laboring breath; first Rustum struck the shield
Which Sohrab held stiff out; the steel-spik'd spear
Rent the tough plates, but fail'd to reach the skin,
And Rustum pluck'd it back with angry groan.

Matthew Arnold (1822–88)

In Snow

O English mother, in the ruddy glow
Hugging your baby closer when outside
You see the silent, soft, and cruel snow
Falling again, and think what ills betide
Unshelter'd creatures,–your sad thoughts may go
Where War and Winter now, two spectre-wolves,
Hunt in the freezing vapour that involves
Those Asian peaks of ice and gulfs below.
Does this young Soldier heed the snow that fills
His mouth and open eyes? or mind, in truth,
To-night, his mother's parting syllables?
Ha! is't a red coat?–Merely blood. Keep ruth
For others; this is but an Afghan youth
Shot by the stranger on his native hills.

William Allingham (1824–89)

In Flanders Fields

IN FLANDERS FIELDS the poppies blow
Between the crosses row on row,
That mark our place; and in the sky
The larks, still bravely singing, fly
Scarce heard amid the guns below.

We are the Dead. Short days ago
We lived, felt dawn, saw sunset glow,
Loved and were loved, and now we lie
In Flanders fields.

Take up our quarrel with the foe:
To you from failing hands we throw
The torch; be yours to hold it high.
If ye break faith with us who die
We shall not sleep, though poppies grow
In Flanders fields.

John McCrae (1872–1918)

A Private

This ploughman dead in battle slept out of doors
Many a frozen night, and merrily
Answered staid drinkers, good bedmen, and all bores:
"At Mrs Greenland's Hawthorn Bush," said he,
"I slept." None knew which bush. Above the town,
Beyond 'The Drover', a hundred spot the down
In Wiltshire. And where now at last he sleeps
More sound in France-that, too, he secret keeps.

Edward Thomas (1878–1917)

Lights Out

I have come to the borders of sleep,
The unfathomable deep
Forest where all must lose
Their way, however straight,
Or winding, soon or late;
They cannot choose.
Many a road and track
That, since the dawn's first crack,
Up to the forest brink,
Deceived the travellers,
Suddenly now blurs,
And in they sink.
Here love ends,
Despair, ambition ends,
All pleasure and all trouble,
Although most sweet or bitter,

Here ends in sleep that is sweeter
Than tasks most noble.
There is not any book
Or face of dearest look
That I would not turn from now
To go into the unknown
I must enter and leave alone
I know not how.

The tall forest towers;
Its cloudy foliage lowers
Ahead, shelf above shelf;
Its silence I hear and obey
That I may lose my way
And myself.

Edward Thomas (1878–1917)

Youth in Arms III: Retreat

This is not war – oh it hurts! I am lame.
A thorn is burning me.
We are going back to the place from which we came.
I remember the old song now: –

  Soldier, soldier, going to war,
  When will you come back?

Mind that rut. It is very deep.
All these ways are parched and raw.
Where are we going? How we creep!
Are you there? I never saw –

Damn this jingle in my brain.
I'm full of old songs – Have you ever heard this?

  All the roads to victory
  Are flooded as we go.
  There's so much blood to paddle through,
  That's why we're marching slow.

Yes sir; I'm here. Are you an officer?
I can't see. Are we running away?
How long have we done it? One whole year,
A month, a week, or since yesterday?

Damn the jingle! My brain
Is scragged and banged –

Fellows, these are happy times;
Tramp and tramp with open eyes.
Yet, try however much you will,
You cannot see a tree, a hill,
Moon, stars or even skies.

I won't be quiet. Sing too, you fool.
I had a dog I used to beat.
Don't try it on me. Say that again.
Who said it? Halt! Why? Who can halt?
We're marching now. Who fired? Well. Well.
I'll lie down too. I'm tired enough.

Harold Monro (1879–1932)

Youth in Arms IV: Carrion

It is plain now what you are. Your head has dropped
Into a furrow. And the lovely curve
Of your strong leg has wasted and is propped
Against a ridge of the ploughed land's watery swerve.

You are swayed on waves of the silent ground;
You clutch and claim with passionate grasp of your fingers
The dip of earth in which your body lingers;
If you are not found,
In a little while your limbs will fall apart;
The birds will take some, but the earth will take most of your heart.

You are fuel for a coming spring if they leave you here;
The crop that will rise from your bones is healthy bread.
You died – we know you – without a word of fear,
And as they loved you living I love you dead.

No girl would kiss you. But then
No girls would ever kiss the earth
In the manner they hug the lips of men:
You are not known to them in this, your second birth.

No coffin-cover now will cram
Your body in a shell of lead;
Earth will not fall on you from the spade with a slam,
But will fold and enclose you slowly, you living dead.

Hush, I hear the guns. Are you still asleep?
Surely I saw you a little heave to reply.
I can hardly think you will not turn over and creep
Along the furrows trenchward as if to die.

Harold Monro (1879–1932)

The Face

Out of the smoke of men's wrath,
The red mist of anger,
Suddenly,
As a wraith of sleep,
A boy's face, white and tense,
Convulsed with terror and hate,
The lips trembling ...

Then a red smear, falling ...
I thrust aside the cloud, as it were tangible,
Blinded with a mist of blood.
The face cometh again
As a wraith of sleep:
A boy's face delicate and blond,
The very mask of God,
Broken.

Frederic Manning (1882–1935)

Bombardment

The Town has opened to the sun.
Like a flat red lily with a million petals
She unfolds, she comes undone.

A sharp sky brushes upon
The myriad glittering chimney-tips
As she gently exhales to the sun.

Hurrying creatures run
Down the labyrinth of the sinister flower.
What is it they shun?

A dark bird falls from the sun.
It curves in a rush to the heart of the vast
Flower: the day has begun.

D. H. Lawrence (1885–1930)

I Tracked A Dead Man Down A Trench

I tracked a dead man down a trench,
I knew not he was dead.
They told me he had gone that way,
And there his foot-marks led.
The trench was long and close and curved,
It seemed without an end;
And as I threaded each new bay
I thought to see my friend.

At last I saw his back. He crouched
As still as still could be,
And when I called his name aloud
He did not answer me.

The floor-way of the trench was wet
Where he was crouching dead;
The water of the pool was brown,
And round him it was red.

I stole up softly where he stayed
With head hung down all slack,
And on his shoulders laid my hands
And drew him gently back.

And then, as I had guessed, I saw
His head, and how the crown –
I saw then why he crouched so still,
And why his head hung down.

Walter Lyon (1886–1915)

The Soldier

IF I should die, think only this of me;
   That there's some corner of a foreign field
That is for ever England. There shall be
   In that rich earth a richer dust concealed;
A dust whom England bore, shaped, made aware,
   Gave, once, her flowers to love, her ways to roam,
A body of England's breathing English air,
   Washed by the rivers, blest by suns of home.

And think, this heart, all evil shed away,
   A pulse in the eternal mind, no less
     Gives somewhere back the thoughts by England given;
Her sights and sounds; dreams happy as her day;
   And laughter, learnt of friends; and gentleness,
     In hearts at peace, under an English heaven.

Rupert Brooke (1887–1915)

Fragment

I strayed about the deck, an hour, to-night
Under a cloudy moonless sky; and peeped
In at the windows, watched my friends at the table,
Or playing cards, or standing in the doorway,
Or coming out into the darkness. Still
No one could see me.

I would have thought of them
– Heedless, within a week of battle – in pity,
Pride in their strength and in the weight and firmness
And link'd beauty of bodies, and pity that
This gay machine of splendour'ld soon be broken,
Thought little of, pashed, scattered …

Only, always,
I could but see them – against the lamplight – pass
Like coloured shadows, thinner than filmy glass,
Slight bubbles, fainter than the wave's faint light,
That broke to phosphorous out in the night,
Perishing things and strange ghosts – soon to die
To other ghosts – this one, or that, or I.

Rupert Brooke (1887–1915)

VICTORIA CROSS - GALLERY.
EANT H. RAMAGE, SCOTS GREYS, DASHING OFF
SINGLE-HANDED TO THE
ASSISTANCE OF TROOPER
MAC'PHERSON WHO WAS
SURROUNDED BY 7
RUSSIAN CAVALRY MEN.
(BATTLE OF BALACLAVA 1854)

3.

B·B·

HARRY PAYNE

Into Battle

The naked earth is warm with spring,
And with green grass and bursting trees
Leans to the sun's gaze glorying,
And quivers in the sunny breeze;
And life is colour and warmth and light,
And a striving evermore for these;
And he is dead who will not fight;
And who dies fighting has increase.

The fighting man shall from the sun
Take warmth, and life from the glowing earth;
Speed with the light-foot winds to run,
And with the trees to newer birth;
And find, when fighting shall be done,
Great rest, and fullness after dearth.

All the bright company of Heaven
Hold him in their high comradeship,
The Dog-Star, and the Sisters Seven,
Orion's Belt and sworded hip.

The woodland trees that stand together,
They stand to him each one a friend;
They gently speak in the windy weather;
They guide to valley and ridge's end.

The kestrel hovering by day,
And the little owls that call by night,
Bid him be swift and keen as they,
As keen of ear, as swift of sight.

The blackbird sings to him, "Brother, brother,
If this be the last song you shall sing,
Sing well, for you may not sing another;
Brother, sing"

In dreary, doubtful, waiting hours,
Before the brazen frenzy starts,
The horses show him nobler powers;
O patient eyes, courageous hearts!

And when the burning moment breaks,
And all things else are out of mind,
And only joy of battle takes
Him by the throat, and makes him blind,

Through joy and blindness he shall know
Not caring much to know, that still
Nor lead nor steel shall reach him, so
That it be not the Destined Will.

The thundering line of battle stands,
And in the air death moans and sings;
But Day shall clasp him with strong hands,
And Night shall fold him in soft wings.

Julian Grenfell (1888–1915)

I Have A Rendezvous With Death

I Have A Rendezvous With Death
At Some Disputed Barricade
When Spring Comes Back With Rustling Shade
And Apple Blossoms Fill The Air
I Have A Rendezvous With Death
When Spring Brings Back Blue Days And Fair

It May Be He Shall Take My Hand
And Lead Me Into His Dark Land

And Close My Eyes And Quench My Breath
It May Be I Shall Pass Him Still
I Have A Rendezvous With Death
On Some Scarred Slope Of Battered Hill

When Spring Comes Round Again This Year
And The First Meadow Flowers Appear

God Knows 'Twere Better To Be Deep
Pillowed In Silk And Scented Down
Where Love Throbs Out In Blissful Sleep
Pulse Nigh To Pulse And Breath To Breath
Where Hushed Awakenings Are Dear
But I've A Rendezvous With Death
At Midnight In Some Flaming Town
When Spring Trips North Again This Year
And To My Pledged Word Am True
I Shall Not Fail That Rendezvous

Alan Seegar (1888–1916)

Dead Man's Dump

The plunging limbers over the shattered track
Racketed with their rusty freight,
Stuck out like many crowns of thorns,
And the rusty stakes like sceptres old
To stay the flood of brutish men
Upon our brothers dear.
The wheels lurched over sprawled dead
But pained them not, though their bones crunched,
Their shut mouths made no moan.
They lie there huddled, friend and foeman,
Man born of man, and born of woman,
And shells go crying over them
From night till night and now.
Earth has waited for them,
All the time of their growth
Fretting for their decay:
Now she has them at last!
In the strength of their strength
Suspended—stopped and held.
What fierce imaginings their dark souls lit?
Earth! have they gone into you!
Somewhere they must have gone,
And flung on your hard back
Is their soul's sack
Emptied of God-ancestralled essences.
Who hurled them out? Who hurled?
None saw their spirits' shadow shake the grass,
Or stood aside for the half used life to pass
Out of those doomed nostrils and the doomed mouth,
When the swift iron burning bee

Drained the wild honey of their youth.
What of us who, flung on the shrieking pyre,
Walk, our usual thoughts untouched,
Our lucky limbs as on ichor fed,
Immortal seeming ever?
Perhaps when the flames beat loud on us,
A fear may choke in our veins
And the startled blood may stop.
The air is loud with death,
The dark air spurts with fire,
The explosions ceaseless are.
Timelessly now, some minutes past,
Those dead strode time with vigorous life,
Till the shrapnel called 'An end!'
But not to all. In bleeding pangs
Some borne on stretchers dreamed of home,
Dear things, war-blotted from their hearts.
Maniac Earth! howling and flying, your bowel
Seared by the jagged fire, the iron love,
The impetuous storm of savage love.
Dark Earth! dark Heavens! swinging in chemic smoke,
What dead are born when you kiss each soundless soul
With lightning and thunder from your mined heart,
Which man's self dug, and his blind fingers loosed?
A man's brains splattered on
A stretcher-bearer's face;
His shook shoulders slipped their load,
But when they bent to look again
The drowning soul was sunk too deep
For human tenderness.

⚔ 203 ⚔

They left this dead with the older dead,
Stretched at the cross roads.
Burnt black by strange decay
Their sinister faces lie,
The lid over each eye,
The grass and coloured clay
More motion have than they,
Joined to the great sunk silences.
Here is one not long dead;
His dark hearing caught our far wheels,
And the choked soul stretched weak hands
To reach the living word the far wheels said,
The blood-dazed intelligence beating for light,
Crying through the suspense of the far torturing wheels
Swift for the end to break
Or the wheels to break,
Cried as the tide of the world broke over his sight.
Will they come? Will they ever come?
Even as the mixed hoofs of the mules,
The quivering-bellied mules,
And the rushing wheels all mixed
With his tortured upturned sight.
So we crashed round the bend,
We heard his weak scream,
We heard his very last sound,
And our wheels grazed his dead face.

Isaac Rosenberg (1890–1918)

Extract from God! How I Hate You

God! how I hate you, you young cheerful men,
Whose pious poetry blossoms on your graves
As soon as you are in them ...
   Hark how one chants –
'Oh happy to have lived these epic days' –
'These epic days'! And he'd been to France,
And seen the trenches, glimpsed the huddled dead
In the periscope, hung on the rusty wire:
Choked by their sickly foetor, day and night
Blown down his throat: stumbled through ruined hearths,
Proved all that muddy brown monotony
Where blood's the only coloured thing. Perhaps
Had seen a man killed, a sentry shot at night,
Hunched as he fell, his feet on the firing-step,
His neck against the back slope of the trench,
And the rest doubled between, his head
Smashed like an eggshell and the warm grey brain
Spattered all bloody on the parados ...
Yet still God's in His Heaven, all is right
In this best possible of worlds ...

Arthur Graeme West (1891–1917)

Back to Rest

A leaping wind from England
The skies without a stain,
Clean cut against the morning
Slim poplars after rain,
The foolish noise of sparrows
And starlings in a wood –
After the grime of battle
We know that these are good.

Death whining down from Heaven,
Death roaring from the ground,
Death stinking in the nostril,
Death shrill in every sound,
Doubting we charged and conquered –
Hopeless we struck and stood.
Now when the fight is ended
We know that it was good.

We that have seen the strongest
Cry like a beaten child,
The sanest eyes unholy,
The cleanest hands defiled,
We that have known the heart blood
Less than the lees of wine,
We that have seen men broken,
We know man is divine.

W. N. Hodgson (1893–1916)

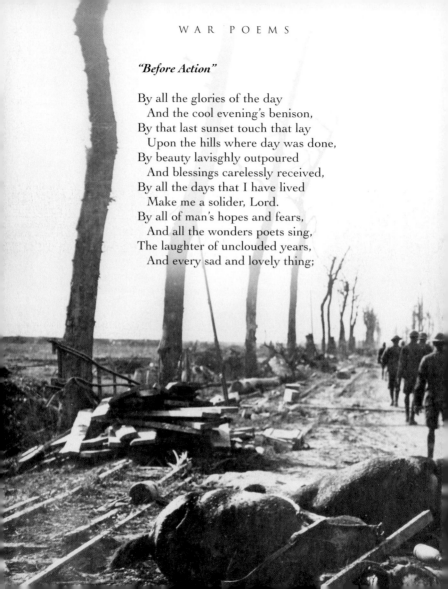

"Before Action"

By all the glories of the day
  And the cool evening's benison,
By that last sunset touch that lay
  Upon the hills where day was done,
By beauty lavisghly outpoured
  And blessings carelessly received,
By all the days that I have lived
  Make me a solider, Lord.
By all of man's hopes and fears,
  And all the wonders poets sing,
The laughter of unclouded years,
  And every sad and lovely thing;

By the romantic ages stored
    With high endeavor that was his,
By all his mad catastrophes
    Make me a man, O Lord.
I, that on my familiar hill
    Saw with uncomprehending eyes
A hundred of Thy sunsets spill
    Their fresh and sanguine sacrifice,
Ere the sun swings his noonday sword
    Must say goodbye to all of this;–
By all delights that I shall miss,
    Help me to die, O Lord.

W. N. Hodgson (1893–1916)

Anthem for Doomed Youth

What passing-bells for these who die as cattle?
  – Only the monstruous anger of the guns.
  Only the stuttering rifles' rapid rattle
Can patter out their hasty orisons.
No mockeries now for them; no prayers nor bells;
  Nor any voice of mourning save the choirs, –
The shrill, demented choirs of wailing shells;
    And bugles calling for them from sad shires.

What candles may be held to speed them all?
  Not in the hands of boys, but in their eyes
Shall shine the holy glimmers of good-byes.
  The pallor of girls' brows shall be their pall;
Their flowers the tenderness of patient minds,
And each slow dusk a drawing-down of blinds.

Wilfred Owen (1893–1918)

Dulce Et Decorum Est

Bent double, like old beggars under sacks,
Knock-kneed, coughing like hags, we cursed through sludge,
Till on the haunting flares we turned our backs
And towards our distant rest began to trudge.
Men marched asleep. Many had lost their boots
But limped on, blood-shod. All went lame; all blind;
Drunk with fatigue; deaf even to the hoots
Of disappointed shells that dropped behind.

GAS! Gas! Quick, boys!– An ecstasy of fumbling,
Fitting the clumsy helmets just in time;
But someone still was yelling out and stumbling
And floundering like a man in fire or lime.–
Dim, through the misty panes and thick green light
As under a green sea, I saw him drowning.

In all my dreams, before my helpless sight,
He plunges at me, guttering, choking, drowning.

If in some smothering dreams you too could pace
Behind the wagon that we flung him in,
And watch the white eyes writhing in his face,
His hanging face, like a devil's sick of sin;
If you could hear, at every jolt, the blood
Come gargling from the froth-corrupted lungs,
Obscene as cancer, bitter as the cud
Of vile, incurable sores on innocent tongues,—
My friend, you would not tell with such high zest
To children ardent for some desperate glory,
The old Lie: Dulce et decorum est
Pro patria mori.

Wilfred Owen (1893–1918)

Spring Offensive

Halted against the shade of a last hill,
They fed, and, lying easy, were at ease
And, finding comfortable chests and knees
Carelessly slept. But many there stood still
To face the stark, blank sky beyond the ridge,
Knowing their feet had come to the end of the world.

Marvelling they stood, and watched the long grass swirled
By the May breeze, murmurous with wasp and midge,
For though the summer oozed into their veins
Like the injected drug for their bones' pains,
Sharp on their souls hung the imminent line of grass,
Fearfully flashed the sky's mysterious glass.

Hour after hour they ponder the warm field —
And the far valley behind, where the buttercups
Had blessed with gold their slow boots coming up,
Where even the little brambles would not yield,
But clutched and clung to them like sorrowing hands;
They breathe like trees unstirred.

Till like a cold gust thrilled the little word
At which each body and its soul begird
And tighten them for battle. No alarms
Of bugles, no high flags, no clamorous haste —
Only a lift and flare of eyes that faced
The sun, like a friend with whom their love is done.
O larger shone that smile against the sun, —
Mightier than his whose bounty these have spurned.

So, soon they topped the hill, and raced together
Over an open stretch of herb and heather
Exposed. And instantly the whole sky burned
With fury against them; and soft sudden cups
Opened in thousands for their blood; and the green slopes
Chasmed and steepened sheer to infinite space.

Of them who running on that last high place
Leapt to swift unseen bullets, or went up
On the hot blast and fury of hell's upsurge,
Or plunged and fell away past this world's verge,
Some say God caught them even before they fell.

But what say such as from existence' brink
Ventured but drave too swift to sink.
The few who rushed in the body to enter hell,
And there out-fiending all its fiends and flames
With superhuman inhumanities,
Long-famous glories, immemorial shames —
And crawling slowly back, have by degrees
Regained cool peaceful air in wonder —
Why speak they not of comrades that went under?

Wilfred Owen (1893–1918)

Strange Meeting

It seemed that out of battle I escaped
Down some profound dull tunnel, long since scooped
Through granites which titanic wars had groined.

Yet also there encumbered sleepers groaned,
Too fast in thought or death to be bestirred.
Then, as I probed them, one sprang up, and stared
With piteous recognition in fixed eyes,
Lifting distressful hands, as if to bless.
And by his smile, I knew that sullen hall,-
By his dead smile I knew we stood in Hell.

With a thousand pains that vision's face was grained;
Yet no blood reached there from the upper ground,
And no guns thumped, or down the flues made moan.
"Strange friend," I said, "here is no cause to mourn."
"None," said that other, "save the undone years,
The hopelessness. Whatever hope is yours,
Was my life also, I went hunting wild
After the wildest beauty in the world,
Which lies not calm in eyes, or braided hair,
But mocks the steady running of the hour,
And if it grieves, grieves richlier than here.
For by my glee might many men have laughed,
And of my weeping something had been left,
Which must die now I mean the truth untold,
The pity of war, the pity war distilled.
Now men will go content with what we spoiled,
Or, discontent, boil bloody, and be spilled.

They will be swift with swiftness of the tigress.
None will break ranks, though nations trek from progress.
Courage was mine, and I had mystery,
Wisdom was mine, and I had mastery:
To miss the march of this retreating world
Into vain citadels that are not walled.
Then, when much blood had clogged their chariot-wheels,
I would go up and wash them from sweet wells,
Even with truths that lie too deep for taint.
I would have poured my spirit without stint
But not through wounds; not on the cess of war.
Foreheads of men have bled where no wounds were.
I am the enemy you killed, my friend.
I knew you in this dark: for so you frowned
Yesterday through me as you jabbed and killed.
I parried; but my hands were loath and cold.
Let us sleep now... "

Wilfred Owen (1893–1918)

Two Sonnets

I

SAINTS have adored the lofty soul of you.
Poets have whitened at your high renown.
We stand among the many millions who
Do hourly wait to pass your pathway down.

You, so familiar, once were strange: we tried
To live as of your presence unaware.
But now in every road on every side
We see your straight and steadfast signpost there.

I think it like that signpost in my land
Hoary and tall, which pointed me to go
Upward, into the hills, on the right hand,
Where the mists swim and the winds shriek and blow,
A homeless land and friendless, but a land
I did not know and that I wished to know.

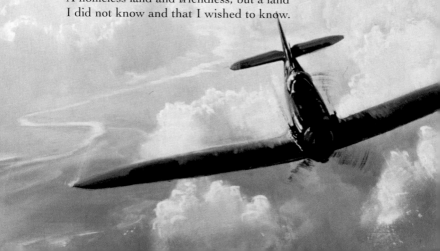

II

Such, such is Death: no triumph: no defeat:
Only an empty pail, a slate rubbed clean,
A merciful putting away of what has been.

And this we know: Death is not Life effete,
Life crushed, the broken pail. We who have seen
So marvellous things know well the end not yet.

Victor and vanquished are a-one in death:
Coward and brave: friend, foe. Ghosts do not say,
"Come, what was your record when you drew breath?"
But a big blot has hid each yesterday
So poor, so manifestly incomplete.
And your bright Promise, withered long and sped,
Is touched; stirs, rises, opens and grows sweet
And blossoms and is you, when you are dead.

Charles Hamilton Sorley (1895–1915)

When You See Millions of the Mouthless Dead

When you see millions of the mouthless dead
Across your dreams in pale battalions go,
Say not soft things as other men have said,
That you'll remember. For you need not so.
Give them not praise. For, deaf, how should they know
It is not curses heaped on each gashed head?
Nor tears. Their blind eyes see not your tears flow.
Nor honour. It is easy to be dead.
Say only this, "They are dead." Then add thereto,
"yet many a better one has died before."
Then, scanning all the overcrowded mass, should you
Perceive one face that you loved heretofore,
It is a spook. None wears the face you knew.
Great death has made all this for evermore.

Charles Hamilton Sorley (1895–1915)

225

RETURNING FROM WAR

Will He No Come Back Again?

Royal Charlie's now awa,
Safely owre the friendly main;
Mony a heart will break in twa,
Should he ne'er come back again.
Will you no come back again?
Will you no come back again?
Better lo'ed you'll never be,
And will you no come back again?

Mony a traitor 'mang the isles
Brak the band o' nature's law;
Mony a traitor, wi' his wiles,
Sought to wear his life awa.
Will he no come back again?
Will he no come back again?
Better lo'ed he'll never be,
And will he no come back again?

The hills he trode were a' his ain,
And bed beneath the birken tree;
The bush that hid him on the plain,
There's none on earth can claim but he.
Will he no come back again?
Will he no come back again?
Better lo'ed he'll never be,
And will he no come back again?

by Al

Whene'er I hear the blackbird sing,
Unto the e'ening sinking down,
Or merl that makes the woods to ring,
To me they hae nae ither soun',
Than, Will he no come back again?
Will he no come back again?
Better lo'ed he'll never be,
And will he no come back again?

Mony a gallant sodger fought,
Mony a gallant chief did fa';
Death itself were dearly bought,
A' for Scotland's king and law.
Will he no come back again?
Will he no come back again?
Better lo'ed he'll never be,
And will he no come back again?

Sweet the lav'rock's note and lang,
Lilting wildly up the glen;
And aye the o'erword o' the sang
Is "Will he no come back again?"
Will he no come back again?
Will he no come back again?
Better lo'ed he'll never be,
And will he no come back again?

Anonymous

An Horatian Ode upon Cromwell's Return from Ireland

The forward youth that would appear
Must now forsake his Muses dear,
   Nor in the shadows sing
   His numbers languishing.

'Tis time to leave the books in dust,
And oil the unusèd armour's rust,
   Removing from the wall
   The corslet of the hall.

So restless Cromwell could not cease
In the inglorious arts of peace,
   But through adventurous war
   Urgèd his active star:

And like the three-forked lightning, first
Breaking the clouds where it was nurst,
   Did thorough his own side
   His fiery way divide:

For 'tis all one to courage high,
The emulous, or enemy;
   And with such, to enclose
   Is more than to oppose.

Then burning through the air he went
And palaces and temples rent;
   And Caesar's head at last
   Did through his laurels blast.

'Tis madness to resist or blame
The force of angry Heaven's flame;
  And if we would speak true,
  Much to the man is due,

Who, from his private gardens, where
He lived reservèd and austere
  (As if his highest plot
  To plant the bergamot),

Could by industrious valour climb
To ruin the great work of time,
  And cast the Kingdom old
  Into another mould.

Though Justice against Fate complain,
And plead the ancient rights in vain —
  But those do hold or break
  As men are strong or weak —

Nature, that hateth emptiness,
Allows of penetration less,
  And therefore must make room
  Where greater spirits come.

What field of all the civil wars
Where his were not the deepest scars?
  And Hampton shows what part
  He had of wise art;

Where, twining subtle fears with hope,
He wove a net of such a scope
  That Charles himself might chase
  To Car'sbrook's narrow case;

That thence the Royal Actor borne
The tragic scaffold might adorn;
  While round the armèd bands
  Did clap their bloody hands.

He nothing common did or mean
Upon that memorable scene,
  But with his keener eye
  The axe's edge did try;

Nor called the Gods, with vulgar spite,
To vindicate his helpless right;
  But bowed his comely head
  Down, as upon a bed.

This was that memorable hour
Which first assured the forcèd power:
  So when they did design
  The Capitol's first line,

A bleeding head, where they begun,
Did fright the architects to run;
  And yet in that the State
  Foresaw its happy fate!

And now the Irish are ashamed
To see themselves in one year tamed:
   So much one man can do
   That does both act and know.

They can affirm his praises best,
And have, though overcome, confest
   How good he is, how just
   And fit for highest trust;

Nor yet grown stiffer with command,
But still in the Republic's hand—
   How fit he is to sway
   That can so well obey!

He to the Commons' feet presents
A Kingdom for his first year's rents,
   And, what he may, forbears
   His fame, to make it theirs:

And has his sword and spoils ungirt
To lay them at the public's skirt.
   So when the falcon high
   Falls heavy from the sky,

She, having killed, no more does search
But on the next green bough to perch,
   Where, when he first does lure,
   The falconer has her sure.

What may not then our Isle presume
While victory his crest does plume?
  What may not others fear,
  If thus he crown each year?

A Caesar he, ere long, to Gaul,
To Italy an Hannibal,
  And to all States not free
  Shall climacteric be.

The Pict no shelter now shall find
Within his particoloured mind,
  But from this valour sad
  Shrink underneath the plaid,

Happy, if in the tufted brake
The English hunter him mistake,
  Nor lay his hounds in near
  The Caledonian deer.

But thou, the War's and Fortune's son,
March indefatigably on
  And for the last effect,
  Still keep thy sword erect:

Besides the force it has to fright
The spirits of the shady night,
  The same arts that did gain
  A power, must it maintain.

Andrew Marvell (1621–78)

The Soldier's Dream

Our bugles sang truce; for the night–cloud had lowered,
And the sentinel stars set their watch in the sky;
And thousands had sunk on the ground overpowered,
The weary to sleep, and the wounded to die.

When reposing that night on my pallet of straw,
By the wolf–scaring fagot that guarded the slain,
At the dead of the night a sweet vision I saw,
And thrice ere the morning I dreamt it again.

Methought from the battle–field's dreadful array
Far, far I had roamed on a desolate track:
'Twas autumn; and sunshine arose on the way
To the home of my fathers, that welcomed my back.

I flew to the pleasant fields traversed so oft
In life's morning march, when my bosom was young;
I heard my own mountain–goats bleating aloft,
And knew the sweet strains that the corn–reapers sung.

Then pledged we the wine–cup, and fondly I swore
From my home and my weeping friends never to part:
My little ones kissed me a thousand times o'er,
And my wife sobbed aloud in her fulness of heart.

"Stay, stay with us – rest, thou art weary and worn:"
And fain was their war–broken soldier to stay;
But sorrow returned with the dawning of morn,
And the voice in my dreaming ear melted away.

Thomas Campbell (1777–1844)

 239

The Caffer Commando

Hark! – heard ye the signals of triumph afar?
'Tis our Caffer Commando returning from war:
The voice of their laughter comes loud on the wind,
Nor heed they the curses that follow behind.
For who cares for him, the poor Kosa, that wails
Where the smoke rises dim from yon desolate vales –
That wails for his little ones killed in the fray,
And his herds by the Colonist carried away?
Or who cares for him that once pastured this spot,
Where his tribe is extinct and their story forgot?
As many another, ere twenty years pass,
Will only be known by their bones in the grass!
And the sons of the Keisi, the Kei, the Gareep,
With the Gunja and Ghona in silence shall sleep:
For England hath spoken in her tyrannous mood,
And the edict is writing in African blood!

Dark Katta is howling: the eager jackall,
As the lengthening shadows more drearily fall,
Shrieks forth his hymn to the hornèd moon;
And the lord of the desert will follow him soon:
And the tiger–wolf laughs in his bone–strewed brake,
As he calls on his mate and her cubs to awake;
And the panther and leopard come leaping along;
All hymning to Hecate a festival song:
For the tumult is over, the slaughter hath ceased –
And the vulture hath bidden them all to the feast!

Thomas Pringle (1789–1834)

I Looked up From my Writing

I looked up from my writing,
  And gave a start to see,
As if rapt in my inditing,
  The moon's full gaze on me.

Her meditative misty head
  Was spectral in its air,
And I involuntarily said,
  'What are you doing there?'

'Oh, I've been scanning pond and hole
  And waterway hereabout
For the body of one with a sunken soul
  Who has put his life–light out.

'Did you here his frenzied tattle?
  It was sorrow for his son
Who is slain in brutish battle,
  Though he has injured none.

'And now I am curious to look
  Into the blinkered mind
Of one who wants to write a book
  In a world of such a kind.'

Her temper overwrought me,
  And I edged to shun her view,
For I felt assured she thought me
  One who should drown him too.

Thomas Hardy (1840–1928)

Extract from The Souls of the Slain

I

The thick lids of Night closed upon me
Alone at the Bill
Of the Isle by the Race –
Many–caverned, bald, wrinkled of face –
And with darkness and silence the spirit was on me
To brood and be still.

II

No wind fanned the flats of the ocean,
Or promontory sides,
Or the ooze by the strand,
Or the bent–bearded slope of the land,
Whose base took its rest amid everlong motion
Of criss–crossing tides.

III

Soon from out of the Southward seemed nearing
A whirr, as of wings
Waved by mighty–vanned flies,
Or by night–moths of measureless size,
And in softness and smoothness well–nigh beyond hearing
Of corporal things.

IV

And they bore to the bluff, and alighted –
A dim–discerned train
Of sprites without mould,
Frameless souls none might touch or might hold –
On the ledge by the turreted lantern, farsighted
By men of the main.

V

And I heard them say "Home!" and I knew them
For souls of the felled
On the earth's nether bord
Under Capricorn, whither they'd warred,
And I neared in my awe, and gave heedfulness to them
With breathings inheld.

VI

Then, it seemed, there approached from the northward
A senior soul–flame
Of the like filmy hue:
And he met them and spake: "Is it you,
O my men?" Said they, "Aye! We bear homeward and hearthward
To list to our fame!"

Thomas Hardy (1840–1928)

The Silence

In the bleak twilight, when the roads are hoar
  And the mists of early morning haunt the down,
His Mother shuts her empty cottage door
  Behind her, in the lane beyond the town:
Her slow steps on the highway frosty white
  Ring clear across the moor, and echo through
The drowsy town, to where the station's light
  Signals the 7.10 to Waterloo.

Some wintry flowers in her garden grown,
  And some frail dreams, she bears with her to–day –
Dreams of the lad who once had been her own,
  For whose dear sake she goes a weary way
To find London, after journeying long,
  The Altar of Remembrance, set apart
For such as she, and join the pilgrim throng
  There, at that Mecca of the Broken Heart.

Princes and Lords in grave procession come
  With wondrous wreaths of glory for the dead;
Then the two minutes smite the City dumb,
  And memory dims her eyes with tears unshed;
The silence breaks, and music strange and sad
  Wails, while the Great Ones bow in homage low;
And still she knows her little homely lad
  Troubles no heart but hers in all the Show.

And when beside the blind stone's crowded base,
   'Mid the rich wreaths, she lays her wintry flowers,
She feels that, sleeping in some far–off place
   Indifference to these interludes of ours,
No solace from this marshalled woe he drains,
   And that the shark Shrine stands more empty here
Than her own cottage, where the silence reigns,
   Not for brief minutes, but through all the year.

Sir John Adcock (1864–1930)

May, 1915

Let us remember Spring will come again
To the scorched, blackened woods, where the wounded trees
Wait with their old wise patience for the heavenly rain,
Sure of the sky: sure of the sea to send its healing breeze,
Sure of the sun. And even as to these
Surely the Spring, when God shall please,
Will come again like a divine surprise
To those who sit to–day with their great Dead, hands in
   their hands, eyes in their eyes,
At one with Love, at one with Grief: blind to the
   scattered things and changing skies.

Charlotte Mew (1869–1928)

Convalescence

From out the dragging vastness of the sea,
Wave–fettered, bound in sinuous, seaweed strands,
He toils toward the rounding beach, and stands
One moment, white and dripping, silently,
Cut like a cameo in lazuli,
Then falls, betrayed by shifting shells, and lands
Prone in the jeering water, and his hands
Clutch for support where no support can be.
So up, and down, and forward, inch by inch,
He gains upon the shore, where poppies glow
And sandflies dance their little lives away.
The sucking waves retard, and tighter clinch
The weeds about him, but the land–winds blow,
And in the sky there blooms the sun of May.

Amy Lowell (1874–1925)

As the Team's Head–Brass

As the team's head–brass flashed out on the turn
The lovers disappeared into the wood.
I sat among the boughs of the fallen elm
That strewed the angle of the fallow, and
Watched the plough narrowing a yellow square
Of charlock. Every time the horses turned
Instead of treading me down, the ploughman leaned
Upon the handles to say or ask a word,
About the weather, next about the war.
Scraping the share he faced towards the wood,
And screwed along the furrow till the brass flashed
Once more.
The blizzard felled the elm whose crest
I sat in, by a woodpecker's round hole,
The ploughman said. 'When will they take it away?'
'When the war's over.' So the talk began –
One minute and an interval of ten,
A minute more and the same interval.
'Have you been out?' 'No.' 'And don't want to, perhaps?'
'If I could only come back again, I should.
I could spare an arm, I shouldn't want to lose
A leg. If I should lose my head, why, so,
I should want nothing more...Have many gone
From here?' 'Yes.' 'Many lost?' 'Yes, a good few.
Only two teams work on the farm this year.
One of my mates is dead. The second day
In France they killed him. It was back in March,
The very night of the blizzard, too. Now if
He had stayed here we should have moved the tree.'

'And I should not have sat here. Everything
Would have been different. For it would have been
Another world.' 'Ay, and a better, though
If we could see all all might seem good.' Then
The lovers came out of the wood again:
The horses started and for the last time
I watched the clods crumble and topple over
After the ploughshare and the stumbling team.

Edward Thomas (1878–1917)

Going Back

The night turns slowly round,
Swift trains go by in a rush of light;
Slow trains steal past.
The trains beat anxiously, outward bound.

But I am not here.
I am away, beyond the scope of this turning;
There, where the pivot is, the axis
Of all this gear.

I, who sit in tears,
I, whose heart is torn with parting;
Who cannot bear to think back to the departure platform;
My spirit hears.

Voices of men,
Sound of artillery, aeroplanes, presences,
And more than all, the dead–sure silence,
The pivot again.

There, at the axis
Pain, or love, or grief
Sleep on speed; in dead certainty;
Pure relief.

There, at the pivot
Time sleeps again.
No has–been, no here–after, only the perfected
Silence of men.

D. H. Lawrence (1885–1930)

Girl to Soldier on Leave

I love you – Titan lover,
My own storm–day' Titan.
Greater than the son of Zeus,
I know whom I would choose.

Titan – my splendid rebel –
The old Prometheus
Wanes like a ghost before your power –
His pangs were joys to yours.

Pallid days arid and wan
Tied your soul fast.
Babel-cities' smoky tops
Pressed upon your growth

Weary gives. What were you
But a word in the brain's ways,
Or the sleep of Circe's swine?
One gyve holds you yet.

It held you hiddenly on the Somme
Tied from my heart at home.
O must it loosen now? I wish
You were bound with the old old gyves.

Love! You love me – your eyes
Have looked through death at mine.
You have tempted a grave too much.
I let you – I repine.

Isaac Rosenberg (1890–1918)

Mental Cases

Who are these? Why sit they here in twilight?
Wherefore rock they, purgatorial shadows,
Drooping tongues from jaws that slob their relish,
Baring teeth that leer like skulls' tongues wicked?
Stroke on stroke of pain, – but what slow panic,
Gouged these chasms round their fretted sockets?
Ever from their hair and through their hand palms
Misery swelters. Surely we have perished
Sleeping, and walk hell; but who these hellish?

– These are men whose minds the Dead have ravished.
Memory fingers in their hair of murders,
Multitudinous murders they once witnessed.
Wading sloughs of flesh these help less wander,
Treading blood from lungs that had loved laughter.
Always they must see these things and hear them,
Batter of guns and shatter of flying muscles,
Carnage incomparable and human squander
Rucked too thick for these men's extrication.

Therefore still their eyeballs shrink tormented
Back into their brains, because on their sense
Sunlight seems a bloodsmear; night comes blood–black;
Dawn breaks open like a wound that bleeds afresh
– Thus their heads wear this hilarious, hideous,
Awful falseness of set-smiling corpses.
– Thus their hands are plucking at each other;
Picking at the rope-knouts of their scourging;
Snatching after us who smote them, brother,
Pawing us who dealt them war and madness.

Wilfred Owen (1893–1918)

Smile, Smile, Smile

Head to limp head, the sunk–eyed wounded scanned
Yesterday's Mail; the casualties (typed small)
And (large) Vast Booty from our Latest Haul.
Also, they read of Cheap Homes, not yet planned;
For, said the paper, "When this war is done
The men's first instinct will be making homes.
Meanwhile their foremost need is aerodromes,
It being certain war has just begun.
Peace would do wrong to our undying dead, –
The sons we offered might regret they died
If we got nothing lasting in their stead.
We must be solidly indemnified.
Though all be worthy Victory which all bought,
We rulers sitting in this ancient spot
Would wrong our very selves if we forgot
The greatest glory will be theirs who fought,
Who kept this nation in integrity."
Nation? – The half-limbed readers did not chafe
But smiled at one another curiously
Like secret men who know their secret safe.
This is the thing they know and never speak,
That England one by one had fled to France
(Not many elsewhere now save under France).
Pictures of these broad smiles appear each week,
And people in whose voice real feeling rings
Say: How they smile! They're happy now, poor things.

Wilfred Owen (1893–1918)

PEACE AND THE
AFTERMATH OF WAR

Lament of the Frontier Guard

By the North Gate, the wind blows full of sand,
Lonely from the beginning of time until now!
Trees rail, the grass goes yellow with autumn.
I climb the towers and towers to watch out the barbarous land:
Desolate castle, the sky, the wide desert.
There is no wall left to this village.
Bones white with a thousand frosts,
High heaps, covered with trees and grass;
Who brought this to pass?
Who has brought the flaming imperial anger?
Who has brought the army with drums and with kettle-drums?
Barbarous kings.
A gracious spring, turned to blood-ravenous autumn,
A turmoil of wars-men, spread over the middle kingdom,
Three hundred and sixty thousand,
And sorrow, sorrow like rain.
Sorrow to go, and sorrow, sorrow returning.
Desolate, desolate fields,
And no children of warfare upon them,
No longer the men for offence and defence.
Ah, how shall you know the dreary sorrow at the North Gate,
With Rihaku's name forgotten,
And we guardsmen fed to the tigers.

Li Po (701–62)

The Female Exile

November's chill blast on the rough beach is howling,
  The surge breaks afar, and then foams to the shore,
Dark clouds o'er the sea gather heavy and scowling,
  And the white cliffs re'echo the wild wintry roar.

Beneath that chalk rock, a fair stranger re-clining
  Has found on damp sea-weed a cold lonely seat;
Her eyes fill'd with tears, and her heart with repining,
  She starts at the billows that burst at her feet.

There, day after day, with an anxious heart heaving,
  She watches the waves where they mingle with air;
For the sail which, alas! all her fond hopes deceiving,
  May bring only tidings to add to her care.

Loose stream to wild winds those fair flowing tresses,
  Once woven with garlands of gay summer flowers;
Her dress unregarded bespeaks her distresses,
  And beauty is blighted by grief's heavy hours.

Her innocent children, unconscious of sorrow,
  To seek the gloss'd shell or the crimson weed stray,
Amus'd with the present, they heed not to-morrow,
  Nor think of the storm that is gathering today.

The gilt, fairyship, with its ribbon-sail spreading,
  They launch on the salt-pool the tide left behind;
Ah! victims—for whom their sad mother is dreading
  The multiplied mis'ries that wait on mankind!

To fair fortune born, she beholds them, with anguish,
  Now wand'rers with her on a once hostile soil,
Perhaps doom'd for life in chill penury to languish,
  Or abject dependence, or soul-crushing toil.

But the sea-boat, her hopes and her terrors renewing,
O'er the dim grey horizon now faintly appears;
She flies to the quay, dreading tidings of ruin,
All breathless with haste, half-expiring with fears.

Poor mourner! — I would that my fortune had left me
The means to alleviate the woes I deplore;
But, like thine, my hard fate has of affluence bereft me,
I can warm the cold heart of the wretched no more.

Charlotte Smith (1749–1806)

France: An Ode

I

Ye Clouds! that far above me float and pause,
Whose pathless march no mortal may control!
Ye Ocean-Waves! that, wheresoe'er ye roll,
Yield homage only to eternal laws!
Ye Woods! that listen to the night-birds singing,
Midway the smooth and perilous slope reclined.
Save when your own imperious branches swinging,
Have made a solemn music of the wind!
Where, like a man beloved of God,
Through glooms, which never woodman trod,
How oft, pursuing fancies holy,
My moonlight way o'er flowering weeds I wound,
Inspired, beyond the guess of folly,
By each rude shape and wild unconquerable sound!
O ye loud Waves! and O ye Forests high!
And O ye Clouds that far above me soared!
Thou rising Sun! thou blue rejoicing Sky!
Yea, every thing that is and will be free!
Bear witness for me, wheresoe'er ye be,
With what deep worship I have still adored
The spirit of divinest Liberty.

II

When France in wrath her giant-limbs upreared,
And with that oath, which smote air, earth, and sea,
Stamped her strong foot and said she would be free,

Bear witness for me, how I hoped and feared!
With what a joy my lofty gratulation
Unawed I sang, amid a slavish band:
And when to whelm the disenchanted nation,
Like fiends embattled by a wizard's wand,
The Monarchs marched in evil day,
And Britain joined the dire array;
Though dear her shores and circling ocean,
Though many friendships, many youthful loves
Had swoln the patriot emotion
And flung a magic light o'er all her hills and groves;
Yet still my voice, unaltered, sang defeat
To all that braved the tyrant-quelling lance,
And shame too long delayed and vain retreat!
For ne'er, O Liberty! with partial aim
I dimmed thy light or damped thy holy flame;
But blessed the paeans of delivered France,
And hung my head and wept at Britain's name.

III

"And what," I said, "though Blasphemy's loud scream
With that sweet music of deliverance strove!
Though all the fierce and drunken passions wove
A dance more wild than e'er was maniac's dream!
Ye storms, that round the dawning East assembled,
The Sun was rising, though ye hid his light!"
And when, to soothe my soul, that hoped and trembled,
The dissonance ceased, and all seemed calm and bright;
When France her front deep-scarr'd and gory
Concealed with clustering wreaths of glory;

273

When, insupportably advancing,
Her arm made mockery of the warrior's ramp;
While timid looks of fury glancing,
Domestic treason, crushed beneath her fatal stamp,
Writhed like a wounded dragon in his gore;
Then I reproached my fears that would not flee;
"And soon," I said, "shall Wisdom teach her lore
In the low huts of them that toil and groan!
And, conquering by her happiness alone,
Shall France compel the nations to be free,
Till Love and Joy look round, and call the Earth their own."

IV

Forgive me, Freedom! O forgive those dreams!
I hear thy voice, I hear thy loud lament,
From bleak Helvetia's icy caverns sent–
I hear thy groans upon her blood-stained streams!
Heroes, that for your peaceful country perished,
And ye that, fleeing, spot your mountain-snows
With bleeding wounds; forgive me, that I cherished
One thought that ever blessed your cruel foes!
To scatter rage, and traitorous guilt,
Where Peace her jealous home had built;
A patriot-race to disinherit
Of all that made their stormy wilds so dear;
And with inexpiable spirit
To taint the bloodless freedom of the mountaineer–
O France, that mockest Heaven, adulterous, blind,
And patriot only in pernicious toils!
Are these thy boasts, Champion of human kind?

To mix with Kings in the low lust of sway,
Yell in the hunt, and share the murderous prey;
To insult the shrine of Liberty with spoils
From freemen torn; to tempt and to betray?

V

The Sensual and the Dark rebel in vain,
Slaves by their own compulsion! In mad game
They burst their manacles and wear the name
Of Freedom, graven on a heavier chain!
O Liberty! with profitless endeavour
Have I pursued thee, many a weary hour;
But thou nor swell'st the victor's strain, nor ever
Didst breathe thy soul in forms of human power.
Alike from all, howe'er they praise thee,
 (Nor prayer, nor boastful name delays thee)
Alike from Priestcraft's harpy minions,
And factious Blasphemy's obscener slaves,
Thou speedest on thy subtle pinions,
 The guide of homeless winds, and playmate of the waves!
And there I felt thee!—on that sea-cliff's verge,
Whose pines, scarce travelled by the breeze above,
Had made one murmur with the distant surge!
And shot my being through earth, sea, and air,
Possessing all things with intensest love,
O Liberty! my spirit felt thee there.

Samuel Taylor Coleridge (1772–1834)

The Battle of Blenheim

I

It was a summer evening,
  Old Kaspar's work was done;
And he before his cottage door
  Was sitting in the sun,
And by him sported on the green
His little grandchild Wilhelmine.

II

She saw her brother Peterkin
  Roll something large and round,
That he beside the rivulet
  In playing there had found;
He came to ask what he had found,
That was so large, and smooth, and round.

III

Old Kaspar took it from the boy
  Who stood expectant by;
And then the old man shook his head,
  And with a natural sigh,
'Tis some poor fellow's scull, said he,
Who fell in the great victory.

IV

I find them in the garden, for
   There's many here about,
And often when I go to plough,
   The ploughshare turns them out;
For many thousand men, said he,
Were slain in the great victory.

V

Now tell us what 'twas all about,
   Young Peterkin he cries,
And little Wilhelmine looks up
   With wonder-waiting eyes;
Now tell us all about the war,
And what they kill'd each other for.

VI

It was the English, Kaspar cried,
   That put the French to rout;
But what they kill'd each other for,
   I could not well make out.
But every body said, quoth he,
That 'twas a famous victory.

VII

My father lived at Blenheim then,
   Yon little stream hard by,

They burnt his dwelling to the ground
　And he was forced to fly;
So with his wife and child he fled,
Nor had he where to rest his head.

VIII

With fire and sword the country round
　Was wasted far and wide,
And many a childing mother then,
　And new-born infant died.
But things like that, you know, must be
At every famous victory.

IX

They say it was a shocking sight
　After the field was won,
For many thousand bodies here
　Lay rotting in the sun;
But things like that you know must be
After a famous victory.

X

Great praise the Duke of Marlbro' won,
　And our good Prince Eugene.—
Why 'twas a very wicked thing!
　Said little Wilhelmine.
Nay—nay—my little girl, quoth he,
It was a famous victory.

XI

And every body praised the Duke
 Who such a fight did win.
But what good came of it at last? —
 Quoth little Peterkin.
Why that I cannot tell, said he,
But 'twas a famous victory.

Robert Southey (1774–1843)

The Soldier's Funeral

It is the funeral march.I did not think
That there had been such magic in sweet sounds!
Hark! from the blacken'd cymbal that dead tone —
It awes the very rabble multitude,
They follow silently, their earnest brows
Lifted in solemn thought. 'Tis not the pomp
And pageantry of death that with such force
Arrests the sense, — the mute and mourning train,
The white plume nodding o'er the sable hearse,
Had past unheeded, or perchance awoke
A serious smile upon the poor man's cheek
At pride's last triumph. Now these measur'd sounds
This universal language, to the heart
Speak instant, and on all these various minds
Compel one feeling.

But such better thoughts
Will pass away, how soon! and there who here
Are following their dead comrade to the grave,
Ere the night fall, will in their revelry
Quench all remembrance. From the ties of life
Unnaturally rent, a man who knew
No resting place, no dear delights of home,
Belike who never saw his children's face,
Whose children knew no father, he is gone,
Dropt from existence, like the withered leaf
That from the summer tree is swept away,
Its loss unseen. She hears not of his death
Who bore him, and already for her son
Her tears of bitterness are shed: when first

He had put on the livery of blood,
She wept him dead to her.

  We are indeed
Clay in the potter's hand! one favour'd mind
Scarce lower than the Angels, shall explore
The ways of Nature, whilst his fellow-man
Fram'd with like miracle the work of God,
Must as the unreasonable beast drag on
A life of labour, like this soldier here,
His wonderous faculties bestow'd in vain,
Be moulded by his fate till be becomes
A mere machine of murder.

  And there are
Who say that this is well! as God had made
All things for man's good pleasure, so of men
The many for the few! Court-moralists,
Reverend lip-comforters that once a week
Proclaim how blessed are the poor, for they
Shall have their wealth hereafter, and tho' now
Toiling and troubled, tho' they pick the crumbs
That from the rich man's table fall, at length
In Abraham's bosom rest with Lazarus.
Themselves meantime secure their good things here
And dine with Dives. These are they O Lord!
Who in thy plain and simple gospel see
All mysteries, but who find no peace enjoined,
No brotherhood, no wrath denounced on them
Who shed their brethren's blood, — blind at noon day
As owls, lynx-eyed in darkness!

O my God!
I thank thee that I am not such as these
I thank thee for the eye that sees, the heart
That feels, the voice that in these evil days
That amid evil tongues, exalts itself
And cries aloud against the iniquity.

Robert Southey (1774–1843)

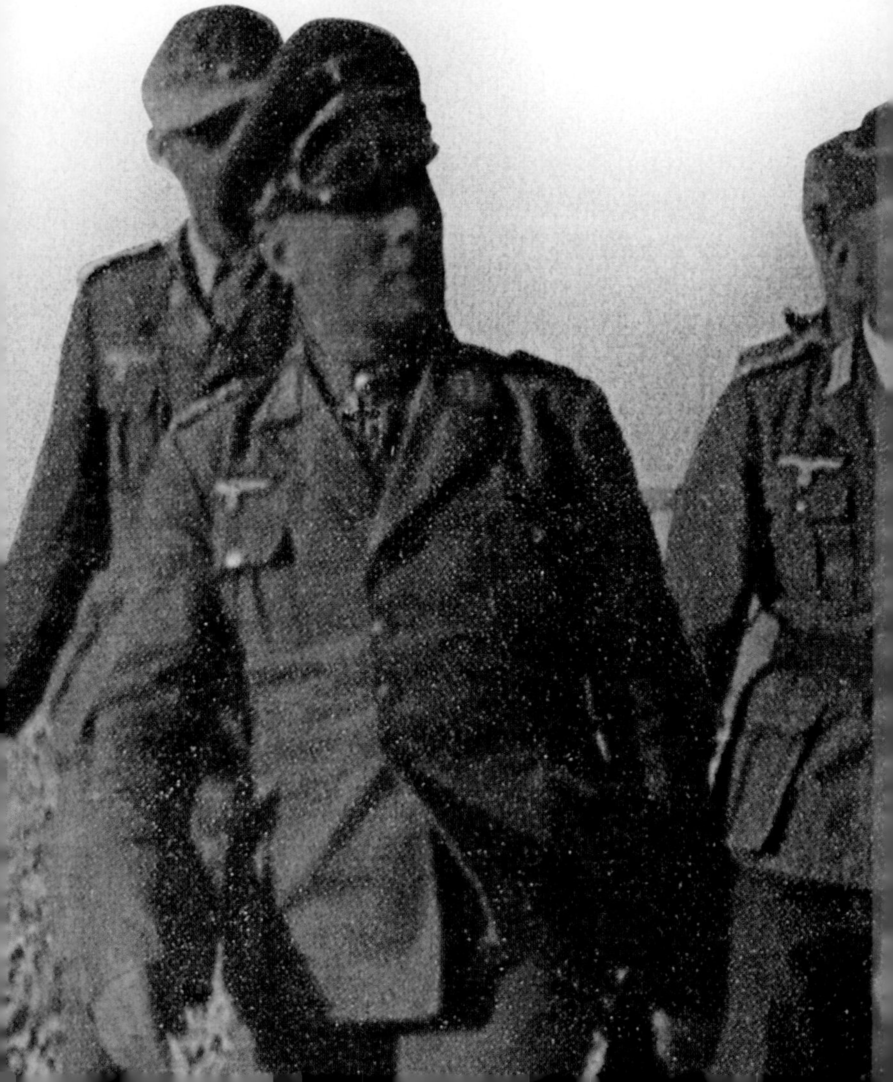

Napoleon's Farewell [from the French]

I

FAREWELL, to the Land where the gloom of my Glory
Arose and o'ershadow'd the earth with her name –
She abandons me now – but the page of her story,
The brightest or blackest, is fill'd with my fame.
I have warr'd with a world which vanquish'd me only
When the meteor of conquest allured me too far;
I have coped with the nations which dread me thus lonely,
The last single Captive to millions in war.

II

Farewell to thee, France! when thy diadem crown'd me,
I made thee the gem and the wonder of earth,
But thy weakness decrees I should leave as I found thee,
Decay'd in thy glory, and sunk in thy worth.
Oh! for the veteran hearts that were wasted
In strife with the storm, when their battles were won –
Then the Eagle, whose gaze in that moment was blasted,
Had still soar'd with eyes fix'd on victory's sun!

III

Farewell to thee, France! – but when Liberty rallies
Once more in thy regions, remember me then, –
The violet still grows in the depth of thy valleys;
Though wither'd, thy tear will unfold it again –
Yet, yet, I may baffle the hosts that surround us,

287

And yet may thy heart leap awake to my voice –
There are links which must break in the chain that has bound us,
Then turn thee and call on the Chief of thy choice!

George Gordon, Lord Byron (1788–1824)

Sonnet to Peace

See, from the fading embers of despair,
  Reviving HOPE beams on the opening day;
And glorious prospects with the new-born year
  ARISE, bedeck'd in all their colours gay.

O'er England's land, lo! angel forms appear,
  Still hov'ring round to guard her sea-girt shore;
And flit triumphant thro' th' expanse of air,
  To welcome PEACE, who visits her once more.

And see, she comes array'd in form divine,
  Led on by FAME and sturdy VICTORY!
On her right hand rich PLENTY rears her shrine,
  And on her left is smiling LIBERTY.

  Sylvans and sea nymphs in the chorus sing,
  While PEACE once more extends her downy wing.

Anonymous (1796)

On the Peace

Earth, cover now the bloody heap!
  Where Albion's gallant warriors lie;
Ye funeral trenches, dark and deep,
Close round their soon forgotten sleep;
  Tis glory's hapless destiny!

Sea, with thy billows, heave the sand
  Around Aboukir's ancient bay,
Lest conscious tempests wash to land,
At angry Nature's wild command,
  The ruins of her fatal day.

And sing your anthems sweet, at eve,
  Ye angels in the listening sky,
The widow's bosom to relieve;
Despair at last may cease to grieve,
  And time may conquer agony.

Her virgin hopes will Peace repair,
  Her love by early sorrows crost;
Her blooming youth consumed with care;
Her pallid cheek no longer fair,
  And happiness for ever lost!

Anonymous (1802)

Reconciliation

Word over all, beautiful as the sky,
Beautiful that war, and all its deeds of carnage, must in time be
    utterly lost,
That the hands of the sisters Death and Night, incessantly softly
wash again, and ever again, this soil'd world;
... For my enemy is dead, a man divine as myself is dead,
I look where he lies, white-faced and still, in the coffin—I draw near,
I bend down, and touch lightly with my lips the white face in the coffin.

Walt Whitman (1819–92)

Extract from When Lilacs Last in the Dooryard

Coffin that passes through lanes and streets,
Through day and night, with the great cloud darkening the land,
With the pomp of the inloop'd flags, with the cities draped in black,
With the show of the States themselves, as of crape-veil'd women,
    standing,
With processions long and winding, and the flambeaus of the night,
With the countless torches lit—with the silent sea of faces, and the
    unbared heads,
With the waiting depot, the arriving coffin, and the sombre faces,
With dirges through the night, with the thousand voices rising
    strong and solemn;
With all the mournful voices of the dirges, pour'd around the coffin,
The dim-lit churches and the shuddering organs—Where amid
    these you journey,
With the tolling, tolling bells' perpetual clang;
Here! coffin that slowly passes,
I give you my sprig of lilac.

Walt Whitman (1819–92)

What the Bullet sang

O JOY of creation,
To be!
O rapture, to fly
And be free!
Be the battle lost or won,
Though its smoke shall hide the sun,
I shall find my love — the one
Born for me!

I shall know him where he stands
All alone,
With the power in his hands
Not o'erthrown;
I shall know him by his face,
By his godlike front and grace;
I shall hold him for a space
All my own!

It is he — O my love!
  So bold!
It is I — all thy love
  Foretold!
It is I — O love, what bliss!
Dost thou answer to my kiss?
O sweetheart! what is this
  Lieth there so cold?

Bret Harte (1839–1902)

A Wife in London

I–The Tragedy

She sits in the tawny vapour
  That the City lanes have uprolled,
  Behind whose webby fold on fold
Like a waning taper
  The street-lamp glimmers cold.
A messenger's knock cracks smartly,
  Flashed news is in her hand
  Of meaning it dazes to understand
Though shaped so shortly:
  He–has fallen–in the far South Land ...

II–The Irony

'Tis the morrow; the fog hangs thicker,
  The postman nears and goes:
  A letter is brought whose lines disclose
By the firelight flicker
  His hand, whom the worm now knows:
Fresh–firm–penned in highest feather –
  Page-full of his hoped return,
  And of home-planned jaunts by brake and burn
In the summer weather,
  And of new love that they would learn.

Thomas Hardy (1840–1928)

Drummer Hodge

They throw in Drummer Hodge, to rest
Uncoffined – just as found:
His landmark is a kopje-crest
That breaks the veldt around:
And foreign constellations west
Each night above his mound.
Young Hodge the drummer never knew –
Fresh from his Wessex home –
The meaning of the broad Karoo,
The Bush, the dusty loam,
And why uprose to nightly view
Strange stars amid the gloam.
Yet portion of that unknown plain
Will Hodge for ever be;
His homely Northern breast and brain
Grow to some Southern tree,
And strange-eyed constellations reign
His stars eternally.

Thomas Hardy (1840–1928)

To Peace, with Victory

I could not welcome you, oh! longed-for peace,
Unless your coming had been heralded
By victory. The legions who have bled
Had elsewise died in vain for our release.

But now that you come sternly, let me kneel
And pay my tribute to the myriad dead,
Who counted not the blood that they have shed
Against the goal their valor shall reveal.

Ah! what had been the shame, had all the stars
And stripes of our brave flag drooped still unfurled,
When the fair freedom of the weary world
Hung in the balance. Welcome then the scars!

Welcome the sacrifice! With lifted head
Our nation greets dear Peace as honor's right;
And ye the Brave, the Fallen in the fight,
Had ye not perished, then were honor dead!

You cannot march away! However far,
Farther and faster still I shall have fled
Before you, and that moment when you land,
Voiceless, invisible, close at your hand
My heart shall smile, hearing the steady tread
  Of your faith-keeping feet.

First at the trenches I shall be to greet;
There's not a watch I shall not share with you;
But more—but most—there where for you the red,
Drenched, dreadful, splendid, sacrificial field lifts up
Inflexible demand,
  I will be there!

My hands shall hold the cup.
My hands beneath your head
Shall bear you—not the stretcher bearer's—through
All anguish of the dying and the dead;
With all your wounds I shall have ached and bled,
Waked, thirsted, starved, been fevered, gasped for breath,
Felt the death dew;
And you shall live, because my heart has said
To Death

  That Death itself shall have no part in you!

Corrine Roosevelt Robinson (1861–1933)

Slain

Dulce et decorum est pro patria mori

You who are still and white
   And cold like stone;
For whom the unfailing light
   Is spent and done;

For whom no more the breath
   Of dawn, nor evenfall
Nor Spring, nor love, nor death
   Matter at all;

Who were so strong and young
   And brave and wise,
And on the dark are flung
   With darkened eyes;

Who roystered and caroused
   But yesterday,
And now are dumbly housed
   In stranger clay;

Who valiantly led,
   Who followed valiantly,
Who knew no touch of dread
   Of that which was to be;

Children that were as nought
  Ere ye were tried,
How have ye dared and fought,
  Triumphed and died!

Yea, it is very sweet
  And decorous
The omnipotent Shade to meet
  And flatter thus.

Thomas William Hodgson Crosland (1865–1924)

The Cenotaph

Not yet will those measureless fields be green again
Where only yesterday the wild sweet blood of wonderful
    youth was shed;
There is a grave whose earth must hold too long, too deep
    a stain,
Though for ever over it we may speak as proudly as we
    may tread.
But here, where the watchers by lonely hearths from the
    thrust of an inward sword have more slowly bled,
We shall build the Cenotaph: Victory, winged, with Peace,
    winged too, at the column's head.
And over the stairway, at the foot—oh! here, leave desolate,
    passionate hands to spread
Violets, roses, and laurel, with the small, sweet, tinkling
    country things
Speaking so wistfully of other Springs,
From the little gardens of little places where son or
    sweetheart was born and bred.
In splendid sleep, with a thousand brothers
To lovers—to mothers
Here, too, lies he:
Under the purple, the green, the red,
It is all young life: it must break some women's hearts to see
Such a brave, gay coverlet to such a bed!
Only, when all is done and said,
God is not mocked and neither are the dead
For this will stand in our Marketplace—
Who'll sell, who'll buy
(Will you or I

Lie each to each with the better grace)?
While looking into every busy whore's and huckster's face
As they drive their bargains, is the Face
Of God: and some young, piteous, murdered face.

Charlotte Mew (1869–1928)

If ye Forget

Let me forget – Let me forget,
I am weary of remembrance,
And my brow is ever wet,
With the tears of my remembrance,
With the tears and bloody sweat,
  Let me forget,

If ye forget – If ye forget,
Then your children must remember,
And their brow be ever wet,
With the tears of their remembrance,
With the tears and bloody sweat,
  If ye forget.

G. A. Studdert Kennedy (1883–1929)

The Dead II

These hearts were woven of human joys and cares,
Washed marvellously with sorrow, swift to mirth.
The years had given them kindness. Dawn was theirs,
And sunset, and the colours of the earth.
These had seen movement, and heard music; known
Slumber and waking; loved; gone proudly friended;
Felt the quick stir of wonder; sat alone;
Touched flowers and furs and cheeks. All this is ended.

There are waters blown by changing winds to laughter
And lit by the rich skies, all day. And after,
Frost, with a gesture, stays the waves that dance
And wandering loveliness. He leaves a white
Unbroken glory, a gathered radiance,
A width, a shining peace, under the night.

Rupert Brooke (1887–1915)

Disabled

He sat in a wheeled chair, waiting for dark,
And shivered in his ghastly suit of grey,
Legless, sewn short at elbow. Through the park
Voices of boys rang saddening like a hymn,
Voices of play and pleasure after day,
Till gathering sleep had mothered them from him.

About this time Town used to swing so gay
When glow-lamps budded in the light blue trees,
And girls glanced lovelier as the air grew dim, –
In the old times, before he threw away his knees.
Now he will never feel again how slim
Girls' waists are, or how warm their subtle hands.
All of them touch him like some queer disease.

There was an artist silly for his face,
For it was younger than his youth, last year.
Now, he is old; his back will never brace;
He's lost his colour very far from here,
Poured it down shell-holes till the veins ran dry,
And half his lifetime lapsed in the hot race
And leap of purple spurted from his thigh.

One time he liked a blood- smear down his leg,
After the matches, carried shoulder-high.
It was after football, when he'd drunk a peg,
He thought he'd better join. – He wonders why.
Someone had said he'd look a god in kilts,
That's why; and maybe, too, to please his Meg,

Aye, that was it, to please the giddy jilts
He asked to join. He didn't have to beg;
Smiling they wrote his lie: aged nineteen years.

Germans he scarcely thought of; all their guilt,
And Austria's, did not move him. And no fears
Of Fear came yet. He thought of jewelled hilts
For daggers in plaid socks; of smart salutes;
And care of arms; and leave; and pay arrears;
Esprit de corps; and hints for young recruits.
And soon, he was drafted out with drums and cheers.

Some cheered him home, but not as crowds cheer Goal.
Only a solemn man who brought him fruits
Thanked him; and then enquired about his soul.

Now, he will spend a few sick years in institutes,
And do what things the rules consider wise,
And take whatever pity they may dole.
Tonight he noticed how the women's eyes
Passed from him to the strong men that were whole.
How cold and late it is! Why don't they come
And put him into bed? Why don't they come?

Wilfred Owen (1893–1918)

Picture Credits

Christie's Images: 156, 169

Image Select: 235, 263

Mary Evans Picture Library: 25, 30–1, 36–7, 84, 96, 155, 171, 195, 197, 200, 226–7, 257, 264–5, 267, 269, 284–5, 296; Edwin Wallace 28–9, 39, 59, 82, 90, 151–3, 158–9, 207, 209, 229, 231, 243, 246–7, 258, 288–9, 294; Explorer Archives 276; Harry Price College, University of London 241; Jeffrey Morgan 16, 63, 66–7, 107, 126, 163, 187, 212, 255, 299; Lucy Pringle 34; National Portrait Gallery 62, 104–5, 134, 137–8, 143–5, 182–3, 225.

The Art Archive Limited: 22–3; Biblotheque Nationale Paris 93–4; British Library 12, 14, 149; Dagli Orti 253; David Shepherd OBE FRSA FRGS/Parachute Regiment–19 250–1; Eileen Tweedy 174; Harper Collins Publishers 19–20; Imperial War Museum 215–6, 293; J.A Brooks/Jarrold/Jarrold Publishing 260–1; Museo del Prado Madrid Album/Josse 280–1; Museum der Stradt Wien/Dagli Orti 270–1, 308; National Army Museum London/Eileen Tweedy 40–1; Private Collection 61, 205; Royal Leicestshire Regiment/Eileen Tweedy 45, 62, 72, 165, 190, 221, 252, 290, 305; Terence Cuneo 80–1, 118.

Topham Picturepoint: 17, 27, 42, 46–9, 51, 55–6, 65, 69, 71–3, 77, 78, 99, 102–3, 108, 110–1, 113, 115, 119, 121, 123, 125, 128–9, 131, 133, 135, 166, 168, 170, 174, 177, 180–1, 185, 188–9, 191–4, 206, 210–1, 213–4, 217, 222–4, 238, 249, 268, 286, 293, 295, 300, 302–3, 307, 309–11, 314–5, 317.

Visual Arts Library: 82

Index of Titles

INDEX

Index of Poets